'Thank God for David Winner. With an easy wit, Winner traces the game back to its roots and the results are as intriguing as they are amusing . . . *Those Feet* really is a marvellous book and you're unlikely to come across anything better for some considerable time.'   *Four Four Two*

'Erudite, witty and utterly unique.'   *Time Out*

'An enchanting love letter to English football . . . It's not really a history, more an attempt to tease out the defining characteristics of English football, its spirit and its style. It's an intriguing journey.'   *Daily Telegraph*

'A slantwise, sparkling and unashamedly clever series of essays.'   *Times Literary Supplement*

'David Winner, the author of the wondrous *Brilliant Orange*, an analysis of Dutch football, has now repeated the manoeuvre in his original and highly individual style with an investigation of the English game. It is a book of surprising twists and turns, casually brilliant flicks and powerful, penetrating insight . . . *Those Feet* is about much, much more than a game.'   *Glasgow Herald*

'It's informed, witty, and always engaging – where else will you find Kundera and Cantona sharing philosophical house room? Think Peter Ackroyd writing the biography of English football and you're half-way there.'   *Metro*

'Highly original . . . There is a wealth of thought-provoking material here which has been too often ignored by less imaginative football writers . . . Winner has an easy, witty, often evocative style.'   *Sunday Telegraph*

'Winner is a witty and intelligent writer with a gift for weaving apparently incongruous strands into a persuasive theory.'   *When Saturday Comes*

'A brilliantly eulogistic book . . . which provides *the* quintessential look at just how mud and leather have helped dictate the rhythms of an Englishman's soul. If you live and breathe the "beautiful game" reading *Those Feet* will do a decent job of helping you understand just why.'   *Ice*

'One of the most ambitious, oddest and most readable books available.'   *Economist*

'More than a football book, this is an examination of the mindset of the English nation, and how it has manifested itself through the game, and Winner's easy style keeps it bouncing along.'   *Irish Times*

'A wonderfully enjoyable read, packed with telling nuggets and dry wit.'   *Daily Telegraph*

'I started reading *Those Feet* just before the World Cup started. I knew it would help me through a summer of disappointment. I loved how he understood tradition was all about the passion and pain – winning can sometimes ruin that.'   GQ

PRAISE FOR *BRILLIANT ORANGE*

'Read of the Year . . . thoughtful, fluent and ambitious – total football writing.' *Independent*

'*Brilliant Orange*. Brilliant book.' *Untold*

'One of the definitive books on the game . . . *Brilliant Orange* is David Winner's inspired extrapolation of the unique character-istics that shape football in the Netherlands.' *The Times*

'A highly original search for the origins of Dutch football culture.' *Financial Times*

'Elegant and thoughtful . . . a genuine attempt to mine the Dutch experience and the various influences – historical, geographic, architectural, artistic – on the Dutch national character, for clues to the unique fact of their footballing near-greatness.' *Times Literary Supplement*

'A highly original celebration and critique of the Dutch masters . . . Winner's disarming enthusiasm and gift for making anarchic but stimulating connections win the day.' *Sunday Times*

'Wry, obsessional, digressive, deep.' *Guardian*

'A witty, pioneering analysis of a country's hopeless confusion between football and national identity.' *New Statesman*

around the world in 90 minutes

around the world in 90 minutes

(+ EXTRA TIME AND PENALTIES)

David Winner

BLOOMSBURY

First published in Great Britain in 2007

Copyright © 2007 by David Winner

The moral right of the author has been asserted

No part of this book may be used or reproduced in any manner whatsoever
without written permission from the Publisher except in the case of brief
quotations embodied in critical articles or reviews.

Bloomsbury Publishing Plc,
36 Soho Square,
London W1D 3QY

Photographs courtesy of the author except where noted otherwise.

A CIP catalogue record for this book
is available from the British Library

ISBN 9780747590835

10 9 8 7 6 5 4 3 2 1

Typeset by Hewer Text UK Ltd, Edinburgh

Printed and bound in Great Britain by Clays Ltd, St Ives plc

Bloomsbury Publishing, London, New York, Berlin

The paper this book is printed on is certified by the © 1996 Forest
Stewardship Council A.C. (FSC). It is ancient-forest friendly.
The printer holds FSC chain of custody SGS-COC-2061.

www.bloomsbury.com/davidwinner

To Momo

the theory

Once upon a time people who liked watching football had to go to a stadium. When there, no two spectators would ever see quite the same thing. Their attention might be drawn to different things on the pitch; each person's vantage point in the stands was unique. All this changed with the coming of television. TV allowed spectators for the first time to share the game in a completely new way. Physical proximity to the players and to other spectators was denied, of course. But the raw material and the story of a game became the same for everyone, just as if they were watching a movie.

This change was profound, but its significance was not immediately realised. For a start, TV pictures, at least initially, were of poor quality. Later, as black-and-white pictures gave way to colour ones, the strange ways in which TV distorted the viewing of a game (replays, slow-mo, the director's sometimes idiosyncratic choice of images and

London, 5 June.

edits) came to be accepted as normal. These days TV's view of football is so ubiquitous that big stadiums routinely offer TV pictures on big screens. The unaided human eye is no longer enough: every significant event in a game must now be confirmed through the electronic eye.

Until the early 1990s, the number of matches shown live was small. That meant most football-lovers still got their fix by visiting a stadium. Then came satellite and cable TV, pay-per-view and the blanket coverage of football. This now exists almost everywhere, and has fundamentally altered the way we experience the game. The pre-satellite era is now as distant to us as silent cinema in the era of the DVD. People still go to stadiums, of course. To do so is prized as the most 'authentic' experience of a match. But, for an increasingly large majority of its burgeoning worldwide audience, top-level football has become something primarily experienced through a TV screen. The old ways have been supplanted: football is now primarily a *virtual* experience. The fans in the stadium serve the same function as the studio audience does in TV shows.

The higher up the food chain, the truer this is. Many more spectators watch Champions League matches on TV than do so in a stadium. And at the game's summit – the World Cup – the number of fans at matches is microscopic compared to the television audience. Up to a million spectators were expected in the stadiums in Germany. But the cumulative TV audience was likely to be even higher than the 28.8 billion FIFA claimed for the 2002 tournament. From a cultural and social – even political – perspective, therefore, the World Cup audience that matters is the one in front of the world's TV sets.

Hence the idea for this book.

The World Cup is now the planet's most important cultural event. Cutting across barriers of language, religion and geography, eclipsing Western pop music and rivalling even the power of Hollywood movies, football has become the world's most potent and popular narrative form. It's a compelling and universally understood drama that makes itself up as it goes along. Indeed, the World Cup generates audience reactions no fiction has ever mustered. Its dramas hold entire nations spellbound. Countries are cast into depression by lost penalty shootouts. Whole populations erupt in wild, spontaneous street parties after famous victories. Think of the mass ecstasies in South Korea 2002, Greece 2004, Cameroon 1990, Argentina 1978 and elsewhere.

Most journalists reckon the place in which to watch the 2006 tournament is Germany. But I think the best place to be is . . . the world.

Instead of merely watching the World Cup – which I can do perfectly well without leaving home – I plan to watch the world watching the World Cup. Starting in Germany, leaving before a ball is kicked, and travelling east through about thirteen or fourteen countries, I hope to watch as many games as possible in the countries taking part – in bars, public places and private homes.

I have no idea what I will discover. Across the continents, will football-watching turn out to be wildly different? Or the same in every place? Will my near-constant jet lag distort my perspective? How will I cope with the 30,000-mile journey? Will my theories about football being a kind of new, universal story for our age survive the encounter with reality? Will I be so tired and culturally confused I no longer care?

I'm about to find out . . .

the practice

Berlin, 6 June 2006 (three days to go)

My idea in coming to Berlin is to leave Berlin. This is my way of saying: I could be here if I wanted, but I reckon the real World Cup is somewhere else. Somewhere Out There.

As soon as I arrive I think I've made a ghastly mistake. I love Berlin, and it's looking even more gorgeous than usual in the chilly sunshine: fresh greenery all around. Buildings gleam. Buses are clean. Even the scratch-iti (usually at plague proportions) is barely evident. S–Bahn trains swish around perfectly. On the other hand, there's a genuinely weird lack of World Cup atmosphere. There's supposed to be some big party tonight for foreign fans up at the Brandenburger Tor. But I was round Berlin all day and I saw hardly anyone wearing shirts. Only very occasionally did I spot even a German flag. Strange. There's commercial stuff, of course. A bus stop beside Dunkin Donuts at Potsdamer Platz has been transformed into a big goal. A giant advert opposite

Burger King near the Zoologischer Garten features a monster-sized footballer in a red shirt and the message promoting friendship through football. The globe/dome thing on top of the Alexanderplatz TV tower, which dominates the city, is a pink and silver football. Looks great. As part of the same campaign pink footballs adorn the top of phone boxes, too. All very wonderful. But what I want to know is: where are the shirts? The flags? The party spirit? The buzz? Totally absent, from what I can tell. Niente. Zip. Nada. Nuffink. London, by contrast, was jumping with World Cup fervour, as if London was about to host six matches, including the final. In London, there were flags everywhere, especially on cars. Not just English ones. Flags from everywhere: Angola, Trinidad, Iran, Portugal, Italy, Mexico, Brazil. Every conversation was dominated by the unlikelihood of Wayne Rooney playing a match. Likewise, in Amsterdam a couple of weeks or so ago, everything was turning orange. But here . . . There's nothing. I thought I might be misreading or imagining this but my friend Julia (lifelong Berliner) confirms it. She calls it 'anti-atmosphere'. She has no theory about why it's like this, though.

I've set myself two tasks today. 1) To go to the Film Museum to see an exhibition about TV and football. 2) To visit the Olympiastadion with Julia, who will take my picture – to prove I really was here.

The exhibition, organised by Petra Schlie (a rare example of a German woman who loves football), explores TV coverage of football through the ages. It tends to reinforce my hunch that the most important things left over from any World Cup are the TV pictures.

I've been to the museum before and found it extra-ordinarily evocative. One of the best things about it is a large room devoted to Marlene Dietrich, with her costumes and possessions in glass cases and her greatest scenes replaying endlessly on a dozen screens. When I see Dietrich I always think of the old lady who lives near my parents in London: the formidable, super-smart Alice Newman, now aged 104, who was at school with Dietrich. Her verdict: 'Marlene was very poor as a student.' Ah, yes, but great at everything else. A smaller room is devoted to the ever-creepy Leni Riefenstahl and the aesthetics of her propaganda film *Olympiad* about the 1936 Olympics, staged, as everyone knows, in the same stadium to host all the Berlin World Cup matches. In the centre of this room is a large model of the stadium as it looked when Riefenstahl used it as a giant prop: no roof or World Cup flags, plenty of swastikas and pride-of-place for the Führer. Petra's exhibition is terrific, too, and features some fantastic TV football clips. Italians and Chileans kicking shit out of each other at the Battle of Santiago in 1962. A breathtakingly boyish Franz Beckenbauer sitting at home in full Bayern Munich strip enjoying Knorr soup *circa* 1966. Gunter Netzer leaping like a salmon after beating Gordon Banks at Wembley. And Zinedine Zidane scoring his amazing last-minute penalty against England in Portugal in 2004. I remark: 'What a guy! First Zidane vomits from sheer nerves – then he takes the most perfect penalty ever seen!'

'*What?*' says Petra.

She's watched the clip a thousand times but never noticed the vomiting part. Wish I hadn't said anything now.

The most bizarre material in room, though, is a clip from Italy's Sunday-afternoon TV football results-and-reports show *Quelli che il Calcio*, featuring a plethora of gorgeous semi-naked girls lap-dancing (more or less) and pole-dancing (more or less) and the latest football scores in small type. The show, which also features comedians, journalists, politicians and football pundits, is Italy's top-rated TV footie extravaganza, and this is Petra's favourite clip. For contrast, she's put it next to the BBC's 'classic', 'solid' *Match of the Day* featuring Mark Lawrenson and Gary Lineker talking about football without any accompanying lap-dancing or pole-dancing.

Petra tells me that her love of football is unusual in Germany and derives in large part from her grandfather, a larger-than-life guy and one-time Cologne footballing legend (and boxer) called Erwin Kohl. Kohl is famous for having punched a referee and getting banned for two years, then being reinstated by Hitler who apparently admired his spirit. 'That's the story, anyway,' says Petra. She also makes intriguing observations about football-as-story. Her favourite thing about football is reading about it in newspapers, especially when Christoph Biermann writes about it in the *Süddeutsche Zeitung*. That, she says, is where the game's characters, narratives, motivations and story arcs come most vividly to life. I ask her about Berlin's lack of World Cup fervour. She reckons it must be because of the long-standing postwar German nervousness (especially in Berlin) about flags and nationalism.

This view is confirmed by my friend Árpád, with whom I'm staying in Schöneberg. A couple of weeks ago he

Berlin, 7 June. Me at Olympic Stadium U-Bahn station.
(picture: Julia Gechter)

decided to stick a small Germany flag on the balcony of
his fourth floor apartment in Gustav-Freytag-Strasse. His
wife Eva thought showing the flag might be too nationalistic.
As a compromise, they decided to go with a small German
flag – and the flags of three other nations they liked: Ghana,
South Korea and USA. This was itself a pretty bold gesture.
No one else in the street is showing any flags at all.

To Olympiastadion, then, with Julia to do the picture.
As we walk up from the U-Bahn station, Julia, who, like
most Berlin schoolchildren, came here to use the Olympic
swimming pool, reflects: 'You can't get away from it; this

really is still a Nazi stadium.' I can't help liking it, though.
It's good architecture. I'd assumed the big space in front
of the stadium would be vibrant with fans, but it's fenced
off. We can't get closer than 400 metres. We try some
pictures at the security fence. Pictures of Julia look great.
Pictures of me look awful. We take some instead at the
U-Bhan station.

We have dinner in a truly awful Italian restaurant at
Savignyplatz, a still-fashionable spot not far from Zoo
station, which is sadder than ever now that a new station,
the Hauptbahnof, has taken most of its passengers. We sit
on the terrace for an hour and a half and there's no World
Cup atmosphere *at all*. A nearby café has World Cup stuff
on its big TV screen. At one point an excited interviewer
interviews Pelé. Pelé says he's very pleased to be in
Germany. The interviewer gets even more excited as he
translates the great man's wise words into German. Around
us, though, there's all the pre-tournament buzz of a grave-
yard. In ninety minutes, we don't see a single person
wearing a World Cup shirt or regalia or hat or anything
. . . In an hour and a half! On the way home later I find
one S-Bahn passenger wearing a *mannschaft* hat, carrying a
little German flag and wearing a 'Germany 2006' T-shirt.
One fan.

berlin

7 June 2006
(D-Day Minus Two)

Almost time for the Big Kick-Off. As far as the world is concerned the first Big One is in Munich: a cheesy opening ceremony, no doubt, followed by Germany–Costa Rica. For me, though, the World Cup will kick off with the Really Big One: Poland–Ecuador. On a big TV screen somewhere to the east. My plan is to watch the game on Friday night in whichever Polish city offers the easiest/cheapest access to Stockholm the following morning (to witness Sweden–Trinidad).

I hear a rumour that, because of outrageous sums of money demanded and refused, Polish TV will not have the broadcast rights to show the World Cup. No problem. I have visions of football-loving Poles clustered round their radios like in the 1930s. I'll go anyway. Ryanair turns out to have a flight to Stockholm (cost: one euro) from Gdańsk's Lech Wałęsa International Airport on Saturday lunchtime. Perfect. I'd thought that my Polish

Oslo airport.

destination would be Kraków or Warsaw, but Gdańsk might be even be better. Yes! Gdańsk. Legendary city of . . . errm, something or other. It comes back. Gdańsk, a.k.a. Danzig, as in 'Danzig Corridor', demanded and then invaded by Hitler, triggering World War Two. Later, Gdańsk was where the Solidarity trade union emerged and broke the back of communism. (Hence Lech Wałęsa International Airport.) I experience a sense of history rushing at me and picture a bleak, melancholy, remote post-Soviet town. I book the flight. On the Net, I discover that the reality is now different. Gdańsk looks like a Baltic version of Bruges. The one-time Hanseatic League port seems to have become something of a tourist trap. But if it was good enough to launch global apocalypse and deliver a mortal blow to communism, it should be good enough to start my World Cup. My journey proper will begin here.

Bizarrely, the quickest, cheapest route from Berlin to Gdańsk turns out to be a flight through Oslo, many hundreds of kilometres the wrong way. Norway failed to qualify for the World Cup. Never mind. I won't have time to see more than a few hills near the airport anyway. I book everything, including a room at the Holiday Inn, Gdańsk, which promises a super-fast Internet connection in every room. Yay! On my way!

world cup

I haul my bags down the four flights of stairs in Árpad's building, then down Gustav-Freytag-Strasse, past the Turkish phone shop and the cake shop. From there, it's down Dominicusstrasse to Schöneberg S-Bahn station for the train to the airport. I love the whooshing sound of the S-Bahn. When I first came to Berlin I'd ride the trains for hours at night, up and down past the neon-lit Alexander-platz, and the angel from *Wings of Desire*, and the Reichstag, and all the other places . . . just for the pleasure of the whooshing, and the watching of Berlin's late-night life. By the time I reach the station with my heavy bags, my shoulder hurts and I realise I need a second piece of luggage, with wheels.

I'm cheered, though, to see belated evidence of World Cup enthusiasm: a total of three black, red and gold Deutschland flags! There's one outside a sex shop, another in front of a sports café and the third on an apartment balcony. On the train I chat in broken-biscuits English to a wizened citizen of former communist East Berlin. As she gets off she says, apropos of nothing that has gone before: 'Give my regards . . . *to ze Kveen!*' I have a boring journey and a two-hour delay in Oslo, where I manage to buy a lovely wheeled suitcase at the duty-free shop. It rolls so smoothly it's like not having luggage. Best of all, says the woman in the shop, if it breaks *anywhere in the world* I can bring it back to Oslo and get a full refund. On the plane I sit next to a Polish builder called Jacek, returning home after building a house for some Norwegians. Jacek confirms what I heard in Berlin: rumours that Polish TV will not show the World Cup are untrue. His son-in-law, experiencing his first-ever plane journey, stares out of the window with amazement at the views below.

Lech Wałęsa International Airport turns out to be only slightly bigger than a bus stop. It gleams with newness and local pride. Relatives of home-coming passengers line a long window on the top floor and wave wildly as their loved ones step on to Polish soil. Gdańsk suddenly becomes, briefly, the centre of my world. A taxi from the City Plus Hallo Taxi company whisks me along a brand-new motorway, past shopping malls, electronics superstores and tramways. I check in to my hotel. Gdańsk is freezing. It's past midnight by the time I go for a late-night walk to explore the old city. Great place! Atmospheric. Pretty. I discover that the correct pronunciation of Gdańsk is 'G-daisk', which would rhyme with 'ice' if ice had a 'k' at the end. I enjoy a delicious plate of chips from a Turkish kebab shop. There are loads of red–and–white Polish World Cup flags on build-ings: simple 'Polska 2006' in red on a white background are the most popular. I discover a funky café called Bazylia on the edge of a square commemorating King Jan III Sobieski, famous for defeating the Turks at the Battle of Vienna in 1683. Behind the bar, a guy called Lucas promises that this will be a fine place to watch the match tomorrow.

Something about the atmosphere makes me believe him. I resolve to return.

'the game is not the point'

Gdańsk, 9 June 2006
Munich 6 p.m. – Germany 4 Costa Rica 2
Gelsenkirchen 9 p.m. – Poland 0 Ecuador 2

Communications from the Holiday Inn are a problem. I try to call Valeria from my English mobile, but a voice tells me: 'You are not allowed to call this number.' Calling from my room is prohibitively expensive, and Skype calls are impossible because the hotel's Internet system does not work. There is a wireless system – but I'll need to buy a scratchcard to access it. So I go to reception.

'Can I buy an Internet wireless scratchcard?'

'We are sold out.'

'I need a scratchcard because your Internet system doesn't work.'

'I know. That is why we are sold out of scratchcard.'

'Can I buy a scratchcard somewhere else?'

'Maybe is possible.'

'Where?'

'At Orange shop near cinema.' [Directions follow.]

At the Orange shop near the cinema, the simple process

Café Bazylia, Gdańsk

of buying a fifteen-euro scratchcard is reminiscent of old ways rather than vibrant post-communism. I must queue in two different queues, each for twenty minutes. From the faces of people around me, I sense they are used to queues. Out of the window, overlooking the Gothic, redbrick railway station, white-and-red trams trundle by, there's a giant crucifix on a nearby hilltop, and all is dominated by a colossal Soviet-era office block at the end of the street. I finally reach the counter where an official fills out a form. I engage him in football chat. He doesn't really like football but he hopes Poland will be better than in the last World Cup, when they were dreadful. He prints four copies of a document. I must now take these copies to the cashier. Another queue. Eventually I hand over my documents and złotys to the cashier, who stamps the documents four times and sends me back to the official who doesn't like football . . . who finally hands over the scratchcard! The whole process has taken about an hour. Back at the hotel, the card works!

In the afternoon I get a daylight taste of Gdańsk. Tourist bits include gabled seventeenth-century houses, smashed by the Nazis during the war and lately rebuilt. There are plenty of art galleries, shops selling amber (the region is famous for it, apparently), cafés along the old docks, a cathedral full of schoolchildren. Away from the centre I find bleak housing and industrial grime. The place I really want to see is the former Lenin Shipyard. From near the hotel, I ask a taxi driver to take me to the former Lenin Shipyard. The driver says the journey will cost the equivalent of about fifteen euros. I agree. One hundred metres later I realise we are passing the former Lenin Shipyard. I should have looked on the map.

Never mind. Gdańsk is, in effect, the birthplace of modern Poland. The low, brick barrack-like shed near the entrance to the shipyards, once the strike headquarters, explains why. It houses a permanent exhibition about the 1980 Solidarity strike, which was triggered by high food prices but went on to challenge – and put the skids under – communist rule in Poland. The place turns out to be remarkably moving. The garden around the building features dozens of contemporary photographs of the strike and music and sounds of the time relayed on loudspeakers. There's even an armoured car from the period, which successfully conveys a sense of what the strikers were up against. Previous anti-communist protests in Gdańsk had been met with gunfire and mass arrests. In a glass case is the bullet-riddled leather jacket of one protestor killed in 1970. But in 1980 the government lost its nerve and surrendered to the strikers, who were inspired in large part by their Catholic faith and the presence in the Vatican of a new Polish pope. The following year a new communist leader, hard-man General

Wojciech Jaruzelski, broke the agreement, imposed martial law and suppressed Solidarity. But the damage to communism had already been done. In 1989, Solidarity negotiated the end of communist government in Poland. Soon afterwards, the Wall fell.

Today, huge cranes are visible beyond the trees on the skyline. There are the sounds of sparse traffic and industrial hammering. Workers from the morning shift, some in Poland football shirts, clock off and head for homes and bars. The grassy area outside the museum is intensely atmospheric and includes huge photographs of the 1980 strike. Loudspeakers play a looped tape of voices and songs and sounds of the strike. This place once employed more than 30,000 men. Now Poland's capitalist economy doesn't really need anyone here, but a couple of thousand workers are kept on because no one in Poland wants to pull the plug on so symbolic a place. As a tiny, belated gesture of solidarity with Solidarity I buy from the modest gift shop a Solidarnosc T-shirt and a Solidarnosc pin. I resolve to wear them for tonight's game.

I go back to the hotel. Phone Valeria. Go out to get something to eat – grilled fish in a restaurant near the water – and wander round Gdańsk, savouring the building pre-match atmosphere, especially in a square near the main gate into the Old Town. By six o'clock it's time for Germany–Costa Rica, the tournament's opening match. I decide to watch this in a nice-looking pub, which turns out to be somewhat quiet and depressing. Near the toilets are murals of Marilyn Monroe and the Beatles from *The White Album*. In the bar there's a big screen but a funereal atmosphere.

Waitresses serve beers as the place gradually fills up with people in Polska scarves and white or red shirts. Germany rattle in goals to sullen near-silence around me. Halfway through, the gloom is beginning to get to me so I leave and head over to Bazylia, which is, as Lucas promised it would be, much livelier, though the place mysteriously empties when the Germany game ends.

The bar's co-owner, a tiny, vibrant, flame-haired twenty-six-year-old called Irena, is unconcerned. The people just departed were mostly tourists. The real crowd – regulars and mates – will come later. She starts setting up for the main event, giving orders as staff clear away tables and set chairs in rows in front of a huge screen and two giant speakers.

About half an hour before the match, Irena's crowd arrives. This comprises about thirty people, most carrying flags and wearing Poland football shirts. In the majority they seem to know each other. They treat me with great friendliness and openness. Irena has the TV sound turned up high. As kick-off approaches, a succession of notables appears on screen. The prime minister, wearing a Poland scarf, predicts a 3–1 win and says that, win or lose, the match will be a test of Polish patriotism. A very old man with curiously intense eyes looks vaguely familiar. Oh my god! It's Lato, one of the great wingers from the 1974 team. He is cautiously optimistic. Two chefs wearing chef outfits explain what the Poland team will have eaten in preparation for the match. The noise in the pub is building. The people around me start to sing and chant. A man comes over to me to predict a 2–0 victory. In Gelsenkirchen, the teams make their way on to the pitch. All around me, wild applause and fervent chanting: Polska! Polska! Polska! When the Polish anthem is played, everyone in the bar stands up and sings. The TV sound is turned up even louder. The game begins! There is incredible noise and emotion in the pub. Every Polish forward pass or throw-in generates shouts and screams. Eyes glisten. There is laughter, shouting, drinking. As the match develops, though, it's obvious that Ecuador are no pushovers. In fact, they're running Poland ragged. Ecuador score. Poland are terrible. Four years ago Poland were humiliated in Korea and came home without winning a match. The crowd in the pub begin to worry about a repeat.

Even so, spirits remain impressively high. The passion and emotion in the pub is remarkable. At half-time there is widespread feeling that Poland will play better in the second half and turn the game around. Irena had devoted much time, effort and money to create the perfect football-on-TV experience. The screen is deliberately huge, the sound loud. 'I wanted it like a theatre or a cinema, to make it more intense,' she explains. In other pubs it may be acceptable to eat, talk and occasionally glance at the TV screen. But for Irena and the Bazylia crowd, *intensity* is essential. 'At the end probably some people will be crying. But it has to be this way. Any other way is pointless. Any other way and it's just a game.' Even so, sharing the experience is much more important than either winning or losing. 'The game is not the point – the point is that we are all together.'

In the second half, Poland get worse. Ecuador, fitter,

stronger, more skilful and tactically superior, dominate. In the pub, the noise level does not drop. It changes, to reflect anguish rather than joy. The faces around me become fixed in expressions of distress. Beside me is a man who has been doing some of the loudest shouting. His white-and-red shirt features a Polish eagle and the words 'Polska Super Fans'. Yet, when Ecuador score a second goal, he does something weird. He raises his arms and punches the air in triumph. His girlfriend, outraged, shouts at him. I ask him why he celebrated. He says: 'At least now we know how the story ends.' By the end Poland have been humiliated. The man who predicted a 2–0 Poland victory comes over again: 'You see? I was right about the score.' The expressive faces in the pub reveal shock, grief, despair. Irena puts on music to lift the mood: Franz Ferdinand's 'Take Me Out'. Very loud. She starts handing out cherry vodkas. She gets up on a table and starts dancing. Everyone joins in. Within five minutes of horrendous defeat, a fantastic party is under way. Everyone is dancing on the tables now. Shouting, whooping. Pretty girls ask me to pose for pictures with them. Soon, everyone is happily drunk. I'd really love to stay, but I've got to get to Stockholm in the morning. As I walk back to the hotel, I realise that what I have just witnessed has been replicated all over the city. From every bar, on every street, people are spilling out and having a party. Gdańsk is full of happy drunks.

gdańsk

10 June 2006
Frankfurt 3 p.m. – England 1 Paraguay 0
Dortmund 6 p.m. – Trinidad & Tobago 0 Sweden 0
Hamburg 9 p.m. – Argentina 2 Ivory Coast 1

Oh shit. I wake with pain and illness. Food poisoning. You really don't want the details. I'm feeling awful. Mainly I'm worried: is this trip over before it has even begun? Is all the planning and anxiety and stress and expectation of the last few weeks to be flushed away by a stupid bacterium? I figure my best chance of keeping things on track is get away from Poland, lay up in calm Stockholm with Tore and Sara and Shuting (who I think of pretty much as family even though we've never met) and take things from there. Several hours and half a truckload of Imodium tablets later I'm in a taxi, stuck in traffic on the road to the airport. On Thursday night the journey took about fifteen minutes. Now it's more like an hour. I'm suddenly less charmed by Gdańsk. I manage not to keel over at check-in. Lech Wałęsa Airport hasn't got automated baggage handling, so I drag the big bag to near the plane. I make it to the departure lounge, surprisingly rich in its supply of toilets. I find the

Gdańsk, 9 June. Irena dances
on the table.

Swedishness of the passengers gathering around me surprisingly reassuring. On the plane I feel vile, but, approaching southern Sweden, the sight is exhilarating. Perfect clear blue skies and dark water – and, suddenly, islands. Dozens of them! Hundreds! Dots and oblongs. Some craggy, some with pine trees and little beaches . . . As far as the eye can see! So beautiful! As if God had decided one day to sprinkle fragments of land into the ocean much as we might sprinkle fish food into a goldfish bowl. By the time we touch down at Skavsta I've decided that life is good after all. The trip, I am sure, will continue.

Skavsta, a true Ryanair airport, is almost absurdly remote. Surrounded by trees and hills and neat farmland; almost two hours from Stockholm. But blessedly calm and clean. On the tarmac, attending the only other plane, I spot a baggage-handler sunning himself and wearing a Viking helmet in Sweden colours, blue and yellow. I make it through customs in time to see England start against

Skavsta airport, 10 June. Baggage-handler wearing Viking helmet in Swedish colours.

Paraguay. After a few seconds Beckham's cross leads to an own goal. I calculate that England will go on to win this easily and I'd rather get into Stockholm than stay here for two hours. I'll catch all the England goals later. There's a radio on the bus, so I spend the journey listening to the Swedish commentary. Surprisingly, I understand entire chunks. Once you get used to the accent, Swedish seems a cross between English and Dutch. I hear a phrase that sounds like 'along the back line' followed by a list of England defenders. I take a wild guess and picture the ball being played along the back line by England defenders. For much of the first half the game seems to consist almost entirely of this manoeuvre. As we drone through the neat Swedish countryside a disappointingly small number of England chances come and go. At half-time Swedish radio plays the worst World Cup song ever recorded, Tony Christie's World Cup version of 'Is This the Way to Amarillo?' Later, I realise the song was the best bit of the match. But I don't mind. Because coming to Stockholm isn't really for the football. Football is just the excuse. This is more of an emotional journey. Unfinished business. Or unstarted business. Some sort of business. To explain: Tamar, one of the loves of my life, who died of cancer five years ago, used to live here with her ex-husband, Tore, and his daughter (her stepdaughter), Sara. And, in all the years before and since, we've never met, though we often spoke on the phone. I always liked the sound of Tore. But somehow we've never come face to face, not even in Jerusalem in the months when Tamar was dying and his visits and mine failed to overlap. Last week Myra, Tamar's mum, gave me his number. He was surprised when I called to say I might pass through Stockholm. He invited me to stay.

Eventually the countryside gives way to some kind of industrial zone, then suburbs, then an endless tunnel . . . and finally the spectacular watery city centre. Tamar used to love the water. Tore comes to the bus station to meet me, a task made easier by mobile phones. Taller, slimmer and greyer than I'd imagined (he was older than Tamar), he's strong, twinkly and reserved. If he were a teacher or a priest in a certain kind of novel, he'd be 'kindly'. He shepherds me through the vast T–Centralen station towards the metro. I find a burst of energy from somewhere. Around us young Swedish men in yellow Sverige team shirts are heading for pubs and public screens, but most passengers on the train are women. In Sweden, says Tore, watching football remains a predominantly male activity. Thankfully, we're not going to a pub. We're going to watch the game at home, with Shuting, his Chinese partner. The last complete game Tore watched was back in 1994, during that year's World Cup, when Sweden reached the semis. I mention Tamar two or three times on the journey, and more later, but Tore quickly switches the conversation. This is not what I imagined would happen, but it's fine. When I meet Shuting I'm slightly stunned by how much she resembles Tamar. Same kind of looks, a similar way of feeling things deeply, a strong and unusual intelligence.

The apartment, in a former school building in a car-free street, has high ceilings and is decorated in a style I used to think was uniquely Tamar's but now realise was influenced by Tore. In every corner and on every wall are books. Books, books, books, in many languages, everywhere and on every subject. In the Ps alone, there's politics, pedagogy, philosophy, psychology. There's plant life in abundance, too, along the window, on tables and shelves, growing with vigour from large earthen pots on the floor. And plenty of clocks, the nicest being a grandfather clock whose ticking manages to be both sonorous and soothing. Knick-knacks everywhere. A paper dragon over the kitchen. The office has six computers. Yet all is harmonious; there's no sense of clutter. It's perfect

Feng Shui. I'm feeling weak and lousy, but the calm of the place and the warmth of Tore and Shuting are lifesavers.

It's time for Sweden–Trinidad, which we watch in their bedroom, on a plasma screen on a bookshelf opposite the sofa, the bed, and a big map of China. The pre-match TV build-up is remarkably warm and generous towards Trinidad and Tobago, the smallest nation ever to send a team to the World Cup. A former Trinidad player whose name I fail to catch talks with still-burning anger about being cheated in a qualifying game against Haiti a very long time ago. The game begins with noise and passion in the stadium, and complete quiet from Tore and Shuting. Fine with me. This book should also be about people who don't care about football. Anyway, I'm just happy to be here, and it's sweet of them to watch at all. I attempt to pique their interest by talking about the skills of Zlatan, the star quality of Henrik 'Larshen', and Dwight Yorke's legendary alleged three-in-a-bed tabloid sex romp. Their interest remains unpiqued. Eventually, though, the game generates some heat of its own. Sweden begin badly and stay that way. Excellent! We're all supporting the underdogs anyway. At half-time it begins to dawn on us that Trinidad might get a draw. They hang on! All three of us are delighted. 'That was exciting,' says Shuting at the end, surprised by her own reaction. Despite my saying on the phone that I wouldn't be able to eat a thing, Shuting makes what looks like a fantastic dinner: reindeer meat cooked with rice and wild mushrooms. I manage half a mouthful before nausea overtakes me. I'm shivering now. I have a fever. I need to get to bed.

stockholm

11 June 2006
Leipzig 3 p.m. – Serbia & Montenegro 0 Netherlands 1
Nuremberg 6 p.m. – Mexico 3 Iran 1
Cologne 9 p.m. – Angola 0 Portugal 1

I slept! I feel weak but improved. The fever has gone. Perhaps the wall of granite outside the window has healing qualities. Deer wander there. The sky didn't get properly dark all night – we're so far north. I sip water for breakfast, then, have a slice of toast on the terrace. I puzzle over a newspaper whose headline denounces Sweden's lousy start. I can't work out written Swedish at all. I'm not fit to fly to Rome today. Tore and Shuting say I'm welcome to stay as long as I need. I feel embarrassed by their generosity but decide to stay a day. Tore points out a cartoon in the paper proving his point about Sweden's unfeminised approach to football. A married couple is watching television, the husband strapped to a chair and screaming. As the announcer reports the start of the next World Cup match, the wife turns off the TV. Ha ha. The afternoon game is Mexico–Iran. But Sara is coming over to meet me; I'd much rather spend time with her. It's hard to believe

Stockholm, 11 June. Sara during Angola–Portugal.

but she is thirty now. And very fine. Blazing with passion, energy, earnestness. She works for NGOs around the world, specialising in dangerous places. Recent assignments include Sudan and the West Bank. To the distress of her extended family in Israel, especially Myra, she has become critical of Israeli policies towards Palestinians.

We all go for a walk down through nearby woods to a lake. The sun is perfect, the pine-scented air is perfect, the water is clear and perfect. Tore and Shuting head back. Sara and I find a rock beside a little beach by the water. Children splash and bask, Muslim families cook food. Elderly Swedes look slightly stunned by the warmth and sunshine. It is the first warm day of summer. Yachts and speedboats swish by. A large ferry with big yellow-and-blue Swedish flat at stern. There are islands in the distance. On the far side of the lake is the centre of the city. Sara points in the far distance to the place where her apartment juts almost into the water. I'm pleased when Sara chats happily about Tamar. I recall pictures of another scene beside another beautiful Swedish lake. Tamar had just started her first round of chemotherapy. Her hair had begun to fall out, so she shaved off what was left and went by boat with her mum to one of her favourite islands where she buried the hair.

By the time we get home Mexico have beaten Iran. Good. Dinner (the reindeer, wild mushrooms and rice from last night) is delicious. First solid food all day. Next up, Angola–Portugal. After a while, all I can think is how glad I am that I didn't fly 10,000 miles to see this match *in* Angola. To be interesting to a neutral, Angola would have to play like lions . . . Or score a goal, have a man sent off and have Shaka Hislop as their goalkeeper . . . Or . . . But they don't. Sara asks if I wouldn't mind watching *Titanic* on the other channel. Of course. Of course. The movie is like an iceberg tearing a big hole below the waterline in my idea that football might be a more compelling form of storytelling than Hollywood cinema. While *Angola–Portugal* is unscripted and almost unwatchable, *Titanic* keeps delivering even when you've seen it dozens of times before. Especially the beginning. We watch the sequence which ends with old Rose delivering the line: 'The woman in the drawing is . . . me.' Gulp. The premise, the enigma, the set-up are all timed and delivered so perfectly as to be irresistible. 'Oh God, that gets me every time,' says Sara, who starts to cry. I can't help myself. I cry too.

rome

12 June 2006
Kaiserslautern 3 p.m. – Australia 3 Japan 1
Gelsenkirchen 6 p.m. – USA 0 Czech Republic 3
Hanover 9 p.m. – Italy 2 Ghana 0

The Arlanda Express from T-Centralen is full of business travellers and takes only twenty minutes. My flight to Rome is delayed, which means I see the last half hour of Australia–Japan in a bar in the departure lounge. On the edge of the small crowd an old Japanese man, leaning on a luggage trolley, stares ahead completely motionless as his nation's 1–0 lead turns to 1–3 defeat in the final ten minutes. Already predisposed to like Australia very much, I'm exhilarated by their fight-back. But will the result screw things up for me when I get to Japan? If Japan lose to Croatia, they'll have nothing to play for against Brazil when I'm in Tokyo.

I have a nice flight on a Danish budget airline. A window seat too! When you're coming from the north, the first hints of Rome are villas with swimming pools . . . Then, suddenly, everything in stunning detail: Stadio Olimpico! St Peter's! Termini! Race track! Ring road! Home! At the airport, Valeria is appalled that I've shaved off my beard. She turns away when I try to kiss her.

'I cannot kiss you because I no longer know you,' she says. I argue that she should be pleased because I look younger and tout London prefers me this way. This cuts no ice. I promise to grow the beard back. She still refuses a kiss.

Meanwhile, our football-watching plans for the night are in trouble. My plane was forty minutes late, so, as Valeria guns her little green Fiat Panda up the Via Appia towards Rome, we are reduced to listening to the Italian and Ghanaian anthems on the radio. The match starts. The commentator is fantastic. As the game gets going it sounds like the most exciting in history. It seems that Italy are being muscled out by the stronger, faster Africans but . . . Ooooooooooooooohhh! Luca Toni just missed an open goal. OK . . . So where are we going?

'There's meant to be a big screen at Piazza Cinecittà,' says Valeria. 'But I drove past an hour ago and there isn't anything. If we want to see young people watching football, we should go to San Lorenzo.' San Lorenzo is my favourite bit of Rome, a bar-filled, leftist, studenty district of cramped and shabby streets south of Termini. One summer night a couple of years back, I passed an open door here and saw a huge crowd packed into a tiny room at the Communist Party building. On the wall behind the committee: a giant Soviet flag and an even bigger poster of Lenin heroically addressing the proletarian masses. San Lorenzo is still one of the few places in the centre of the city where people in cafés read books. San Lorenzo it shall be.

The major roads aren't exactly deserted (this is Italy's first game, after all, and it's only Ghana) but I've never seen so few cars around here. At the normally traffic-choked Porta Maggiore ours is the only vehicle. Around the corner, just past a huge new graffito reading 'Fascism: never again', Valeria parks beside the tram tracks. I reckon tonight it's probably safe to leave the computer bag in the boot and we head into San Lorenzo by foot, walking quickly up the narrow road that runs beneath the hefty, ancient, graffiti-besmirched city walls. From almost every window comes the sound of the TV commentary. In one basement a dozen people crowd around a tiny set. We lean in and ask: 'What's the score?' '*Zero a zero.*' Actually, we knew that already, but asking added immensely to our party feeling. We head for the big square beside the church and . . . Bingo!

The Gambrinus pub in Via dei Sabelli has turned a big TV set to face the street where a semicircle of thirty or forty young San Lorenzniks are watching with rapt attention. We soon realise we're not the only ones watching the watchers. A dapper young man in a white linen suit called – strangely enough – Lorenzo is filming the crowd for a local Rome TV station. He doesn't like football. He prefers basketball. He wishes Italians would devote less time and attention to football and focus on the huge problems in the country, many of which he blames on former prime minister Silvio Berlusconi. This is not a party atmosphere like in Gdańsk. Nor is there an iota of the semi-detached, semi-ironic attitudes of London. No. This little crowd is focussed and intense. Apart, perhaps, for a lone Somali man standing back from the crowd, who climbs on to the footrest of a parked Vespa for a better look. The faces of the pub crowd are nervy and fixed on the game. The crowd is tense. The crowd just wants to win. The tension drains away a little when Pirlo slams in a fine first goal. But the real drama comes near the end when Ghana's defender Kuffour underhits a back-pass, allowing Iaquinta to steal in and score the second goal, making the game safe for Italy. A girl beside me dances around with glee, shouting: '*Abbiamo Vinto! Abbiamo Vinto!*' ('We've won! We've won!')

What happens next makes me feel like I'm witnessing something peculiar to this ancient place. The cameras zoom in for a tight close-up on the distraught Kuffour. It's the kind of moment simply unavailable in a stadium. The TV shows Kuffour from an unflattering angle, bent over from behind, prostrate on his knees, head in hands, experiencing the kind of psychological agony that comes only from screwing up on the biggest stage of all. A British TV commentator at this point would say something sympathetic. The Gambrinus crowd do something else. They switch instantly from happy celebration: they start to jeer and abuse Kuffour. They laugh at his pain. They mock him. The moment ends as soon as the TV director switches to Iaquinta and replays of the goal. But here, in the shadow of walls built 1,700 years ago, in a street named after a people destroyed by the armies of Rome, in this place full of happy young fans, I have the feeling I just witnessed an echo of something very old and very dark.

When the game ends, the crowd disperses quickly. No Franz Ferdinand. No cherry vodka. No dancing on tables. Valeria and I hoped there might be some wild, horn-tooting,

Piazza Venezia, Rome. 12 June.

flag-waving Italian communal ecstasy and decide to head in to town to look for it. It doesn't take us long to find it. The streets in the city are coming back to noisy life. Pretty soon the place is buzzing with mopeds, cars and flag-wavers. We drive past the Colosseum, and down Via dei Fori Imperiali. The closer to Piazza Venezia we get, the more intense the celebrations. We drive across to the largest group of revellers and park in what is normally a busy bus stop, right underneath the balcony from which Mussolini addressed the masses in the 1920s and 30s.

Soon we're engulfed in a delirious crowd, everyone waving huge tricolori and making phenomenal noise. The horn of every vehicle in the piazza is hooting. The crowd grows bigger and more restless. Chants go up: 'Forza Italia'; AS Roma songs. A six-year-old girl in teddy-bear pyjamas dances around on a car rooftop as her father, immensely proud, looks on and makes sure she doesn't fall. Traffic in the square is now completely blocked by revellers who begin to (playfully) rock the smaller cars and beat on the windows of buses. Someone produces a flag even bigger than all the others, which becomes a canopy under which cars must now pass. I ask one bare-chested man waving a huge flag why people are so excited. After all, it's only a football match – and it's only Ghana. He looks at me pityingly and says: 'Football is everything.'

rome

13 June 2006
Frankfurt 3 p.m. – South Korea 2 Togo 1
Stuttgart 6 p.m. – France 0 Switzerland 0
Berlin 9 p.m. – Brazil 1 Croatia 0

Past and present are jumbled so profoundly in Rome it's hard to get your bearings. The ancient Forum, for example, is a mess of grey stones, modern roadway, churches, tourists. A better sense of what the ancient city looked like is visible at the fabled Cinecittà Studios, south of the city, on the stupendous $100-million set built for the HBO-BBC TV show *Rome*. Mysteriously, the show has not done justice to its own creation: every shot is filmed so tightly we never see the full majesty of the place. In person, the set (on the very lot where *Ben Hur*, *Cleopatra* and a host of sword-'n'-sandal epics were filmed in the 1950s and 60s) is far more impressive, especially in its full-scale re-creation of the Forum at the time of Caesar. En route to Ciampino (for the flight to London to catch the plane to Korea) I drop in at the studio to see Jonathan Stamp, football-lover, formidable classicist and historical consultant on *Rome*. One of Stamp's themes is how much modern Italian life continues to be massively influenced by its ancient Roman past. I want to ask if that applies to sport, to *calcio*.

Stamp's answer: 'Absolutely!' He goes on to suggests some truly startling parallels between football and what was ancient Rome's favourite sport – chariot-racing.

For example, football fans wave red, white and green flags and wear Italy's blue national shirt. But chariot fans were doing that in the Circus Maximus 2,000 years ago, waving the four big teams' colours – which, by weird coincidence, were red, white, green and blue. Indeed, passions of the ancient *tifosi* put modern fervour in the shade. In 77BC one Reds fan famously threw himself on the funeral pyre of a star rider. As with the *azzurri*, chariot-racing helped a chronically tense and divided country unite around its passion for sport. Racing inspired betting and superstition. Results were followed around the country. Other aspects of modern *calcio* were prefigured by chariot-racing too. The four big chariot teams, known as *factiones*, operated like the mega-rich football clubs of today: huge, money-generating sporting monopolies with powerful political connections. Teams attempted to poach star riders from their rivals. Stars commanded salaries and prize money on a par with today's footballers. And nothing in World Cup 'corporate hospitality' this year will be as high-profile – or as nerve-racking – as the regular visits the emperor Caligula liked to make to his preferred chariot team, the Greens.

Even the social and cultural functions of ancient and modern sport share similarities. Modern football unites Italians of all ranks and status. So did the races. The Circus Maximus was a meeting place between the Patricians of the Palatine Hill and the Plebeians of the Aventine. So chariot races allowed classical Romans meet despite differences in rank, status and gender. The vast audiences for chariot races were even comparable in scale to modern TV audiences for football. The Circus Maximus regularly attracted 250,000 and 300,000 spectators – from a city of one million. (By comparison, top attendance for the Colosseum's gladiator shows was about 80,000 and the largest-ever crowd for a modern football match is 208,000, at the Maracana in Rio.) In other words, one third of the population of ancient Rome turned out for chariot races: the entire city was touched by them. Stamp says: 'These days we are more interested in the grimmer rituals of gladiator contests. But that would have seemed very odd to an ancient Roman. Gladiatorial games were only an occasional feature of Roman life. Chariot-racing was the exact equivalent of modern soccer.'

He also reckons that the ancient-Roman attitude to winning and losing still shapes the Italian mindset. 'If you look at Italy through the glass of ancient Rome, it's always been a culture in which competition is open. Life is about winners and losers. The mantra of the liberal postwar British generation that life was not about winning and losing is utterly meaningless to Italians. They still have the Roman sense that life is a brutal competition. Death or glory. No pity, no mercy if you lose. Adulation if you win. The political system in ancient Rome was called the *cursus honorum*, literally the "race of honours" and a phrase taken directly from the chariot races.'

I ask about the possible antecedents of last night's cruel

jeering of Kuffour. Stamp says it might have been a distant echo from the darkest place of all: 'It may be a kind of residue of radiation from the way Romans behaved in the Colosseum. Those games weren't just gladiators. They featured "highlights", like seeing women raped by animals, slaves murdered by armed soldiers, defenceless criminals put to mass execution and so forth.' A complex psychology was at work among the Romans who enjoyed such shows. 'Most ancient Romans lived in shitty apartment blocks, in places where the roof touched their nose when they lay in bed. They had to scrabble for day-to-day existence. They often lived on the dole, without much self-respect. They were removed from their roots in that they had often grown up on the land or on a farm but had had to move to the city. So their day-to-day existence was pretty fucking miserable. But at the same time they were encouraged to believe that they were in the centre of the world. They were Romans. And the one time I think that had any real meaning for them was when they were up in the stands at the Colosseum and, looking down at some poor schmo being buggered or beheaded or both, they could say: "He's a slave. He's given up his life and dignity, but I'm a Roman and I'm free." There was a powerful sense of self-vindication in being able to say: "At least I'm not him." You feel a vicarious sense of power and dignity and, to fuel that, the victim needs to be humiliated and ultimately killed. In a contemporary context, maybe humiliation is sufficient. Kuffour probably doesn't realise how lightly he got off.'

london

14 June 2006
Leipzig 3 p.m. – Spain 4 Ukraine 0
Munich 6 p.m. – Tunisia 2 Saudi Arabia 2
Dortmund 9 p.m. – Germany 1 Poland 0

I'm missing matches. I'm trying not to, but they sort of slide by as I move from one place to another. It's not only travel that does the damage. In Rome, for example, South Korea–Togo was only available on Sky TV. John doesn't have Sky. And the local cafés didn't show the game either. France–Switzerland? Well, that was my choice. But I thought: I'll be able at least to catch the last game of the day at the airport because Italians adore football and they'll definitely show Brazil's first match (against Croatia). But Ciampino has no screens at all. The only places to sit are the floor or metal benches. And there's no one from the airline to explain the long delay (caused by thunderstorms over southern England). All in all, then, a disappointing evening. A two and-a-half-hour flight turns into a nine-hour journey. Valeria and I arrive in London stressed and perfectly knackered for Thursday's flight to Asia.

You need to know where all this is going, so a word

about the route I worked out with an expert called Abby Hazell at Trailfinders in Kensington High Street, a famous travel agency just yards from one of Kubrick's locations for *A Clockwork Orange* (Alex picked up the girls at the record store there). Back in April, when I first had the idea for this trip, I planned to watch games in each of the five continents. The original itinerary was: London, Berlin, Luanda or Accra, Kiev, Seoul, Sydney, Buenos Aires, Rio, London and a European country for the final. A limited budget, though, meant a drastic rethink. I could do this only with some kind of round-the-world ticket, with limitations of its own. Australia turned out to be a too-arduous and risky detour (and how likely was it that Guus Hiddink would even get Australia to the second round?). Ukraine would have involved a hugely expensive side trip. Ditto Africa. In fact, just about everything about Africa was problematic. One idea was to go to Luanda for Angola's early clash with Portugal (former colony versus former colonists). But the journey would be exceedingly long and ludicrously expensive. And Luanda was in the grip of cholera and violent crime epidemics. Abidjan for Ivory Coast–Holland seemed a fun alternative until the Foreign Office advised that Ivory Coast is one of the two most dangerous destinations on earth (more dangerous than Iraq) and firmly warned against travel of any kind there. Ghana might have been fun and friendly, but the only match to see there would have been against Italy, which looked a certain, comfortable Italy win. The last possibility was Tunis to see Tunisia–Saudi Arabia. That's this afternoon. And going there might have meant missing the only un-missable flight of the entire trip – the one to Seoul tomorrow. Anything going wrong in Tunis, even an hour's delay, would have seen me tossing my Star Alliance round-the-world ticket in the bin.

Thus, the plan for the long-haul world journey now looks like this: South Korea tomorrow night, followed by Japan for Japan's final group-stage game. After that (because the ticket obliges it) I'll detour through Canada and USA for the round of sixteen. And from there to South America for the real action: Argentina in the quarter final and Brazil in the semi. One or both nations are bound to make it that far. Unless Brazil play Argentina in the final, the last leg will be to fly back to Europe and watch the final in whatever European country meets Argentina/Brazil. En route, though, the ticket allows me to change flight timings at will. For a penalty of £75 I can alter the route whenever I need to.

So . . . Early afternoon: to Kensington to pick up tickets from Trailfinders (including the ticket for Valeria, who's coming as far as Tokyo). Abby has gone to Malawi. Trailfinders is vast, like a travel department store. There are several annexes in side streets, too.

Meanwhile it sounds like Spain are playing terrifically well against Ukraine. I'm happy about this because on Australian radio I predicted that Spain would win the World Cup. I didn't really believe this when I said it – I just didn't want to say 'Brazil', like everyone else does. I also figured that a) Spain have good players; b) it's now thirty-one years since the death of Franco (long enough for the poison to have drained from the system); and c) Spanish World Cup luck must surely change one day.

While we wait for our tickets to be printed, we watch the end of the first half and most of the second half in a nearby pub called the Prince of Wales along with two Romanian electricians, Sorin and Gheorghe, waiting to pick up documents from their embassy nearby. Like many London pubs, this one is decorated with flags from every nation for the World Cup. The TV sound is turned down, and pop music is playing. The pub is busy but we're the only people watching the match. When Valeria reveals her Roman identity, the conversation takes a surprisingly archaeological turn. Sorin asks if we know Trajan's Column, depicting the emperor's victory over the Dacians. We do indeed. 'Well, that's us!' he says excitedly. 'We are Dacians!' The Spain game spins by in a dazzle of Romanian pride. For example, do we know which European people speak the language closest to ancient Latin? 'Um, Romanians?' 'Yes!' And which people have the strongest claim to owner-ship of the disputed region of Transylvania? (Clue: it's not Hungarians.) Sorin says that, before the war, Romania was one of the most vibrant and thriving economies in Europe. Ceausescu and communism fucked up Romania. But now it's a fantastic place, and coming up fast. Pretty soon Romania will be in the EU and the euro. He says that Romanian football is not so shabby either. Both he and Gheorghe predict that Romania will do well in the next World Cup. I hope so, for their sakes. Meanwhile, Spain look fantastic: 4–0 in their first match! Am I the king of predictions, or what?

Late afternoon: to Hampstead to buy an extra pair of lightweight trousers for hot countries. Valeria gives me time

off to have coffee and watch the second half of Tunisia–
Saudi Arabia with the Iranian owner of the fabled Coffee
Cup café near Waterstone's on the High Street. The match
is poor but there are at least goals, and the ecstasy of Saudi's
Al Jaber after scoring what appears to be the winning goal
is moving. Then Tunisia score a late equaliser through Jaidi,
prompting the excited English commentator to say something which I suspect would be considered pretty bizarre
down the bazaar: 'That's the first goal scored at the World
Cup by a Bolton Wanderers player since Nat Lofthouse in
1954!'

Tonight, for sentimental reasons, Valeria wants to eat at
Geeta Indian restaurant in Kilburn. I'd prefer to stay in and
watch Poland–Germany. We compromise. We'll have a
leisurely and sentimental chicken tikka masala at Geeta
(during which I'll listen, in one ear only, via headphones,
to the BBC radio commentary). And then we'll go up the
road to a pub to watch the second half. Also, Valeria will
film everything using her Uncle Ezio's video camera,
borrowed and brought all the way from the village in
southern Lazio. I'm still glowing with the spirit of Gdańsk,
so when a car flying four Polish flags appears in the rear-
view mirror I encourage her to film that too. Mysteriously,
the Poles in the car don't recognise this as a gesture of
Solidarnosc. They become angry, stop their car (is it stolen?)
and make threatening gestures. The driver gets out of his
car and heads our way. Valeria improvises, smiles sweetly
and gestures that she was only filming buildings. I drive
off before the Polish driver gets too close. She doubts he
was really Polish. Indian, she thinks. But why would an

Indian drive round London with Polish flags on his stolen car? We reach Geeta and enjoy a delicious and leisurely dinner in the knowledge that very little of interest is happening on the field in Dortmund. Up the road, we find another pub called the Prince of Wales, next to one of the nicest cemeteries in London. Poland are playing with great heart but are struggling to keep out the Germans. Like its Kensington namesake, the Kilburn pub is decorated with the flags of many nations. The three screens are huge but the pub is mostly empty. One of the few people paying full attention to the game is an old man who stares fixedly ahead and moves only one part of his body – his arm, as he raises his beer glass to his mouth and then puts the glass back on the wooden table. Does the game remind him of something in his past?

It used to be axiomatic that when Germany played Anyone in the World Cup, pretty much everyone in England would support the Anyone. To my astonishment, Oliver Neuville's late, late winning goal for Germany is received warmly in the pub. Someone says, 'Yeah, well done the Germans,' and there's even a smattering of applause. The old man says nothing. In the BBC studio, Mark Lawrenson and Alan Hansen are also enthusiastic. They praise the scoring of the late German goal as 'traditional'. They love the passionate German support. They admire Klinsmann's positive approach and the Germans' refusal to settle for the draw. I think I've just witnessed symptoms of a Major Cultural Shift.

Meanwhile, Valeria has become fascinated by the white-and-red St George car flags all over the city. At the late-night

London, 14 June. Germany–Poland.

Tesco store on Willesden Lane we find a bargain: a pair of St George car flags plus plastic flagpoles for just 97p! We invest. Valeria wants to drive round London with a flag. It takes us a while to figure out how the car flags work. First you have to get the little nylon flag on to the stick. Then you attach the little plastic-bobble thing to the end of the plastic stick to stop the flag flying off the stick . . . And then somehow you wedge the stick between the window and the door frame. But it works! The plan is: Valeria wants to take one plastic St George flag back to Italy. The other we will show off around London now, and then donate to my mum (who won't want it). We set off, driving first towards Edgware Road, then past the high-security anti-terrorist police station, then past Marble Arch, and on down Park Lane. Valeria is entranced by the flapping noise the flag makes as the wind catches it. She films the flapping flag from several angles with Ezio's camera. She waves to other cars with flags. They wave back! We have become members of the Fellowship of the Flag. 'I am a Cockney!' says Valeria. There's no denying it. We drive round Hyde Park Corner twice, to get a better look at the building once known as Number One London: the former home of the Duke of Wellington at Apsley House. We head for Buckingham Palace, then Parliament Square. Valeria loves these car tours of tourist London. I warn: 'Don't wind down the window too far in case we lose the flag.' We cross Westminster Bridge. Oh no! As we passed the Mother of Parliaments, Valeria opened the window a fraction too wide and the flag blew away. For security reasons, cars are not allowed to stop on Westminster Bridge, but we have to get the flag back. We turn round, come back, circle Parliament Square, get on to the bridge and pull over. The slightly crumpled little flag is lying on the pavement. The plastic stick is gone but Valeria jumps out and retrieves the flag. She strokes and smoothes it, as if it were a cat. We set off for home.

london

15 June 2006
Hamburg 3 p.m. – Ecuador 3 Costa Rica 0
Nuremberg 6 p.m. – England 2 Trinidad & Tobago 0
Berlin 9 p.m. – Sweden 1 Paraguay 0

It's all building up nicely for the Next Really Big One (England v. Trinidad, of course), which takes place this afternoon. BBC coverage is round-the-clock and exemplary, especially on radio. Items include interviews with the prime minister of Tobago, who happens to be Dwight Yorke's former teacher (he persuaded Yorke out of international retirement), and a sweet, long, live interview from the Caribbean with the father of Shaka Hislop, Trinidad's goal-keeping hero against Sweden. Hislop Snr reveals that he speaks to his son every day. He hopes that Shaka keeps a clean sheet against England. In a strange way we all hope so too. There's a part of most Englishmen that not only roots for the plucky underdog but also secretly wishes for national football humiliation. We enjoy the orgy of right-eous indignation that always follows. Naturally, this is never the case with our club teams. Nor does it happen when England play a proper team like Brazil or Argentina or

Germany. We want to win against them. But an embarrassing performance against a loveable minnow like, say, Trinidad (especially when it does no serious damage to our prospects) is perfectly fine. It gives us a chance to display our anguish. We pretend to be distressed. But the moaning, complaining, rending garments and wondering where the nation went wrong is actually one of the most cherished parts of any World Cup. It shows we care.

To be in plenty of time for the flight to Korea – and in order to watch the game – we will take a minicab to Heathrow. This is because the Tube takes longer (and because a cab will be quicker and cost slightly less than two tickets on the express train from Paddington). But the cab is twenty-five minutes late and the driver arrives in a state of agitation, bitterly denouncing his dispatcher for sending him to the wrong street. He then spends the whole journey complaining: '. . . He don't speak English. No one speak English these days.' I try unsuccessfully to change the subject to football but Valeria observes and listens with open-mouthed fascination.

'London is fantastic!' she says later. 'A person who speaks terrible English complains about the other person who speaks terrible English! Incredible! In London no one speaks English but things works; everyone has a job, everyone makes money. In fact, the people who speak bad English probably do better than the people who speak good English. Look at you: your English is beautiful and you're penniless! In Rome it's the opposite. In Rome anyone who doesn't speak perfect Italian has no chance. But there are no jobs anyway. When I speak Italian, I'm judged. When I speak English at university, I'm judged. It's nice, London.'

We're the first people to check in for the Asiana flight. The assistant is Brazilian. I confess that I'm hoping someone other than Brazil wins the World Cup. She disarms me completely by agreeing. 'Oh yes. We win too many times. And the team is no good. Everyone in Brazil thinks it's OK someone else wins.'

Eh?

No time to ponder that. Let's get upstairs and find a TV. About 300 other people have had the same idea. It's late in the first half and the bar is packed. Every chair taken. Smoke hangs thickly. No chance of getting a drink. People are standing in a huge semicircle around three or four big screens. Being as this is Europe's biggest airport, and this is as international a crowd as you'd find anywhere, a surprising number of people (about half) seem to want England to win. But England are playing horribly. Luckily, a Scottish man called Colin, waiting for a plane to Glasgow, explains what we've missed and why England will fail: 'Most of the first half England were even worse. Complete shite! But then what else can England be? Shite players. Shite manager. Shite tabloids telling them every day how fucking great they are and putting them under impossible pressure by saying they're gonna win the fucking World Cup! The guy I feel sorry for is Eriksson. No, I mean it! Got no fucking chance, has he? What other team in the World Cup has newspapers that build them up and up, talk complete shite all the time, and still go on about 1966? England were bloody lucky to win the World Cup in 1966. And they only bloody did it once. And it was fucking forty years ago. And they still keep fucking going on about it.

But they'll not win it this year. No chance. Just you watch. And not next time either. Or the time after. They're just not good enough. That's the bottom line. And it'll keep happening because your tabloids make life absolutely fucking impossible.' England are indeed poor, but Trinidad's luck can't hold and eventually doesn't. The amiable Crouch, looking increasingly like a cartoon character, loops in a header to break the heart of Shaka Hislop's dad. Gerrard scores from long range. England are through to the second round. Colin stands by every word. 'Well, *of course* they beat Trinidad. So what? You just wait. You'll see how right I am.'

russia, mongolia, china . . . and korea

15 June 2006
Gelsenkirchen 3 p.m. – Argentina 6 Serbia & Montenegro 0
Stuttgart 6 p.m. – Netherlands 2 Ivory Coast 1
Hanover 9 p.m. – Mexico 0 Angola 0

Technically the plane sits on London concrete, but the moment we board the Asiana jumbo at Heathrow we enter another country. The firstest of impressions confirm that Korea will be strange and appealing. There's little of the usual noise and sharp-elbowed behaviour of Westerners getting ready for a crowded eleven-hour flight. Instead, the muted décor and strikingly chic and friendly cabin staff contribute to an air of remarkable calm. A spirit of kindliness prevails as we settle in. Seats seem roomier than usual. We may be flying in what would be cattle class on other airlines but it feels almost luxurious. Valeria loves the plane, is charmed by the stewardesses and the elegance of their uniforms. The sight of Koreans *en masse* reading Korean newspapers triggers a half-remembered early-childhood flashback: frustration, bafflement about how grown-ups know what writing – all lines and dots and squiggles – means. One day I'll know. But I'll never enter the world

of Korean words. Valeria, on the other hand, is almost
already there. She is trying to discover if Korean characters
are similar to Chinese ones. (She studies Chinese.)
Temporarily she is defeated by the squiggles and bubbles.
Meanwhile, I am restricted to the universal language of
TV. On the screens is the in-flight news show, with English
subtitles. Approximately two minutes of the news is devoted
to North Korea's imminent (and highly alarming) ICBM
missile test. But about an hour is given over to in-depth
coverage of South Korea's 'tingling come-from-behind
victory' in the World Cup over Togo a couple of days
ago. Togo's single goal and Korea's two goals are replayed
endlessly. There are lengthy interviews with Korean players
and officials and plentiful images of Dick Advocaat (Korea's
new coach) looking wise and masterful. The Koreans – the
so-called 'Italians of Asia' – have not yet twigged that things
may not go quite so brilliantly with this Dutchman as they
did with Guus Hiddink. But Advocaat looks terrific.

For me, South Korea is somehow the key to this whole
journey. I missed the Korea/Japan experience in 2002. But
watching on TV I was mesmerised by the scenes from
Seoul, the hundreds upon hundreds of thousands of fans,
all wearing identical pink-red shirts, transported by their
team's unexpected surge to the semi-final. I thought: if those
scenes are repeated in 2006, I want to be there. I want to
get up in the middle of the night with them. I want to
see the passion, the hysteria, the weirdness.

Over the last few weeks, of course, I've done a bit of
research. I asked around, I spoke to academics. But the

true nature of new Korean football passion remains elusive
I've heard that the fervour is more nationalistic than that
of, say, Japan. I've heard that the Korean League is feeble
and that it's only the national team that brings out the
millions of fans in red shirts. I've heard that, before the last
World Cup, the Korean population knew so little about
football that evening courses were arranged in cinemas and
schools, teaching them how to behave as fans ('Become
excited when there is a throw-in for the Korea team;
become even more excited when there is a corner for the
Korea team'). Yet, within weeks, Korea's image in the
world and Koreans' sense of their own identity were transformed. Football suddenly strode to centre stage in the
South Korean national drama. How? What does the Korean
experience tell us about the power of the game as ritual,
story, culture?

I doubt that I'll find any deep answers to these questions
in three days (especially as I'll be rendered moronic by jet
lag). But the passion of four years ago will definitely be
repeated. The frenzy has already been going on for weeks.
My friend Árpad was in Seoul a couple of weeks ago and
sent a tantalising email: 'Korea will be one of the most exciting
and strange places of your trip. Koreans are absolutely crazy
about football. But they do not even have the slightest idea
what the game is about. In literally EVERY bar and restaurant
people were watching some absolutely unimportant warm-
up match of the REDS. But they behaved as if it was already
the World Cup. There is a big advertisement campaign with
slogans like "AGAIN 2002" and you see many people wearing
the red or white-and-red national shirts of the team . . .

Every fifty metres you are reminded of the World Cup. It gives us a great feeling of global fever, as if you are really connected with all those billions out in the world who wait for the Cup to start.' He also warned me that everyone gets lost all the time in Seoul. Oh yes – and I should forget that hotel he recommended: it's a dump.

Hurtling east, night comes surreally fast. The lights in the plane go off. Blinds come down. I cheat, lift my blind and glimpse the lights of St Petersburg before cloud covers Russia. Using our new, inflatable travel pillows, we attempt to sleep. For a few minutes we doze. Still hurtling east, the night is unnaturally short. Breakfast involves spicy squid. Beneath us the Gobi Desert, then some other vastness – reddish, bleak, dotted with what look like quarries and chemical works. Mountains. Rivers. Chinese trees, hills, wilderness, farms, roads, towns, cities, coast . . . A sea – the Korean coast! Which looks much bigger than it does on Google.Earth. Meanwhile, strange rituals have been going on for two hours. We were all offered red ginseng face masks. I declined and soon regretted it. Valeria accepted. With her face covered with a kind of wet bandage she looked like a burns victim but went into raptures. 'Oh, it's amazing! Wow! So nice!' Near the stairs, hostesses perform a service for female passengers: putting on make-up. The atmosphere is nurturing and sweet-natured. I'm tired, of course, but this is the nicest eleven-hour flight I can remember.

Incheon Airport is shiny and quiet. There's a waterfall on the way to baggage reclaim. The driver bows to the passengers before we set off, then the 'limousine bus' takes an

age before dropping near a big famous hotel. We get lost
several times on the short walk to our little-known (but
nice) Hyundai Residence Hotel. It's early morning for us,
but here it's evening. The area was advertised as something
of a cultural centre. It's full of motorbike shops and the
smells of oil and fuel. By the time we check in we're
exhausted. A shower. This is something like my seventh
city in nine days. I ask: 'Why are we here?' Valeria says:
'It was your idea.' I'm too tired to think; I forget why I
had the idea. We've got to eat. The guy at the front desk
recommends taking a taxi or subway to a fancy place about
three miles away. We'll take our chances in the nearby fish
market, which is very large and seems to sell nothing but
seaweed and dried squid. Eventually we find a nice-looking
traditional place a street or two away. As we head for the
low tables at the back, everyone shouts out in horror and
points to our feet. We were meant to take our shoes off.
In fact, from the shock on the faces around us, it would
have been less of a gaffe to have brought dead rats to the
table. But they see we're foreign and forgive us almost
immediately. The owner, an elderly woman with spectacular
lilac-dyed hair, a culinary legend in these parts, it turns
out, brings a menu with pictures. We pick cold noodles
with beef and chilli paste. From the next table a doctor
who speaks English advises that foreigners don't usually like
such food. I win him over with my efficient use of chopsticks. The food is great! Our presence is creating a stir.
From the next table, another diner leans in and, via the
doctor, explains that he knows all about Italy. He serenades
Valeria with a medley of Neapolitan songs and snippets

from *La Bohème*. Valeria is astounded by the perfection of his singing. 'Even I don't know these songs. These are the kind of songs my grandmother knows.' The doctor is a philosopher, a cultural critic. We talk about Seoul and the soul of Korea, about China, about the dangerous north, about America, about the passing of Korean traditions. I'm struggling. The doctor offers to drive us around the city in his Mercedes. By now utterly exhausted, we have to say no.

I must try to sleep a few hours before the game. Valeria wakes me at one a.m. for Holland–Ivory Coast. This I must see. The view from our room on the tenth floor is fantastic. Outside one window a cluster of skyscrapers twinkle and ripple like something out of *Blade Runner*. Valeria ostentatiously declines to watch the football, reads a book instead, and then gets busy with the table lamp, trying it in several parts of the room. When I shout at the referee, she shushes me and reminds me that everyone else in the building is sleeping. Robin van Persie is having a tremendous game. Scores with a fantastic free kick! Holland race to a two-goal lead! But the second half is unspeakably tense as the Dutch defence creaks, sways and – eventually – holds out. I feel thoroughly invigorated. Now Holland don't need to beat Argentina – which is just as well, because highlights of Argentina's six-goal victory over Serbia earlier look frightening. One of the goals involves about thirty passes. I suspect my age-old prejudices against Argentina may crumble, especially as the game against them is no longer decisive. José Pekerman: cool. Football: amazing. Fans: adorable. Even Maradona seems nice today, dressed as (and shouting like) an ordinary fan. Forget Spain –

Argentina will win the World Cup. The Korean TV coverage is amiable too. The commentators scream with what seems genuine enthusiasm for every goal and near miss. There are no studio discussions. And, after the Holland match, a mildly amusing lookalikes sequence: Ballack/Matt Damon, Luis Figo/Alec Baldwin, Scolari/Gene Hackman, and Oliver Neuville/Frodo from *Lord of the Rings* . . . Followed, blissfully, by sleep.

pick a time zone

Seoul, 17 June 2006
Frankfurt 3 p.m. – Portugal 2 Iran 0
Cologne 6 p.m. – Czech Republic 0 Ghana 2
Kaiserslautern 9 p.m. – Italy 1 USA 1

Seoul, 16 June 2006 (Or, if I prefer, 17 June. My body clock, time zone and World Cup-match schedule are beginning to disagree violently, so I think I should choose my own date and time. Trouble is, I don't know which one suits me best.)

Seoul feels fractionally less peculiar than it did yesterday (insert 'today' or 'tomorrow' if it helps) but I still have no idea what's going on. We've spent much of the day sight-seeing. Valeria feels the need to see 'sights', as in guide books. To me, everything seems like a sight: the massive subway trains, the big buildings, the mountains inside the city, the bewildering jumble of giant traffic-filled streets with no names, ginseng shops, live fish outside restaurants. Dog shops. Teashops. Electronic hyperstores. White-gloved flunkeys at a department store treated us with prodigious politeness. We visited a palace and a park (I forget which ones). We ate tasty super-spicy food sitting crosslegged on a floor. (I like the water bottles on every table; I'm not so keen on the oval metal chopsticks.) We observed companies of soldiers in brightly coloured ceremonial costumes, looking like movie extras. Most people were friendly and helpful. We enjoyed the big fountains and the hordes of children splashing about. The sun beat down. The humidity was less than we expected. We couldn't work out why some women hide their faces completely with full-visor mirrored sunglasses.

Anyway, all this is just preparation for the Really Really Really Big One, which we hope to experience alongside an estimated half a million screaming Korean kids in the Seoul City Hall Plaza in the middle of the night — four a.m. local — or tonight or today or tomorrow. (From now on, you choose.) That's right: South Korea–France! My biggest game so far. France will win easily, of course, but that's not the point. Then again, what is the point? Is it going to be a festival of national chauvinism? It doesn't quite feel like that. A monster party like a New Year's Eve? Closer. Semi-religious rite? Could be.

Meanwhile, entering into the spirit (and because in some parts of the city there's nothing else for sale) I've equipped myself with a) a cardboard fan (for keeping away middle-of-the-night heat) which reads: 'Victory Korea! Korea Victory!'; b) a red Nike 'Go Korea!' plastic bracelet; c) an electric nylon (but it did cost only 7,000 won) red Korea team shirt which reads 'Shebangs! Korea!'; and d) a red, white, black, blue, yellow and white Korea flag baseball hat. Valeria will trump me — *ovviamente* — by wearing a little all-black outfit with a pair of clip-on devils' horns on her head (the team is known as Red Devils).

The man who sold me the baseball hat asked if I was

from America. 'England,' I corrected. He beamed and said: 'Ah, England! David Beckhambauer!' Which was almost exactly right. At the Lotte Mart mega supermarket at Seoul Station every single one of the twenty checkout girls wears an identical Korean football shirt. Near the entrance to the Myung Dong subway station a giant screen is showing highlights again and again and again of Korea's amazing unexpected triumphs at the 2002 World Cup. First the penalty victory over Spain, then the even more stunning win against Italy. Few of the hundreds of teenagers milling about are watching. They are more interested in the penalty-taking competition on stage. But a tiny, wiry old man – old enough to have personally witnessed the last two destructions of the city – is watching rapt. As Ahn scores again his incredible winning goal the old man's face becomes a mask of extreme ecstasy. His eyes roll backwards. His eyelids flutter. His mouth opens wide in a silent scream . . . After a few seconds he returns to the present and sees me watching him. He reaches out his hand. I take his hand. He squeezes my hand and speaks intense-sounding words in Korean which I do not understand. Then he whispers in English: '*Blue!*'

I smile and try to reciprocate: 'Blue.'

'*Bluuuu!*' he hisses and points to the screen. He clenches his fist and points again:

'*Bluuuu!*'

Aaaaaahhh – I get it! Not blue but Les Bleus! The *Blues*. He has entered into an altered state in order to make a mystic prediction. He is telling me that the Korean team will beat France.

seoul

17–18 June 2006

Nuremberg 3 p.m. – Japan 0 Croatia 0
Munich 6 p.m. – Brazil 2 Australia 0
Leipzig 9 p.m. – France 1 South Korea 1

We plan to be up all night, so we try to sleep in the afternoon – but can't. Never mind: adrenaline will work just as well. The TV build-up started hours ago with a variety show including a theatre full of people in red shirts waving Korean flags. On stage, semi-naked dancing girls. And singers. And what songs! My favourite, thumped out by a black-belt soprano, went: 'Fifa! Fifa! Fifa! Fifa! Fifa World Cup!!!' On KBS1 still the shows roll on . . . Right now schoolgirls, dressed all in white with red trim, singing. The audience is still waving Korea flags.

The game will start at four a.m. and it's now seven p.m. The weather is warm. Visibility is perfect. So first stop will be Namsan, the mountain that looms over the centre of the city. On top of Namsan is Seoul Tower, a Berlin-style TV mast which is Seoul's favourite landmark. The top is the best bit: probably no structure in any city anywhere in the galaxy affords a more spectacular view. We get a taxi to take us most of the way to the summit. Just hearing the whine of the engine is tiring. Near the top, a jogger nips past us, not even sweating. The secret of South Korea's success in 2002 was the team's almost insane levels of fitness, which allowed them to outrun and outfight more skilful opponents. A theme of the Korean press in recent weeks has been that the energy and dynamism of the young, thrusting dynamic Red Devils mirrors the energy and dynamism of the young, thrusting Korean economy. The French, positively *ancien* by comparison, may be ripe for the picking . . .

Most visitors reach Namsan by cable car. On this balmy Sunday night the place hums with sightseers, the great majority of them Korean and most wearing Korean team shirts. The pre-match buzz is palpable, carnivalesque and playful. The atmosphere is sexy rather than nationalistic. Languid, devil-horn-wearing couples entwine in quiet corners or pose for pictures against the spectacular setting. Two girls and a boy throw jokey poses amid a stand of plastic trees that have footballs instead of leaves. From the top of the tower Seoul trembles with lights, split in two by the thunderous blackness of the Han River, further bisected by molten streams of traffic along the great avenues. In American cities, any one of the clusters of tall brightly lit buildings would be 'downtown'. Seoul has downtowns as far as the eye can see.

Now it's eight o'clock – eight hours before kick-off. I point one of the viewing platform's electronic telescopes towards Seoul City Hall Plaza. We plan to get there just after midnight, which should give us loads of time to stroll around and pick a nice spot to watch the game. I'm shocked: the square is already full. I panic. 'What if we can't get in?'

Valeria soothes: 'Listen to yourself. Get in to where? It's a big open space with screens. There'll be space for everybody. It will be fine.' I'm struck that the virtual experience of joining with others to watch a match on TV has begun to mimic characteristics once reserved for stadiums alone. Two months ago in Nottingham I saw pubs selling tickets for the pubs' screenings of England World Cup games. Reports from Fan Mile in Berlin suggest that the same process is taking place in Germany. The physical locations of matches are increasingly peripheral. The real action, the emotional focus (the key cultural phenomenon) is now in front of big screens. I knew this would happen in the home countries. I'm surprised it's also happening in Berlin, practically within shouting distance of Olympiastadion. There seem to be more fans on the Mile (and having a better time) than spectators at the stadium.

We take the cable car down from Namsan mountain. Valeria grips my hand tightly. The swaying, rapid descent makes other passengers nervous, too. The car swings over a tree-studded void and people go 'Woooooo'. I remember the cable car in *Where Eagles Dare* and figure we're not on the roof fighting with an ice-pick-wielding maniac, so why worry? Safely at the bottom, we walk through old winding streets towards Namdaemum to find food. The Sinpo Woori Mandoo restaurant is not full, but most of the other customers are like us: just getting ready for the match. There are couples, groups of women adjusting make-up, putting on face paint. They look cute in their horns. No one pays much attention to the day's first match (Croatia–Japan). It's a pre-clubbing atmosphere. We're going to a party!

On the menu, octopus looks good. Turns out to be the hottest thing I've ever attempted to eat. I give up on octopus and order soup, salad, noodles and beef instead. Pickles, too, for balance. We are fuelled! By now, pretty much everyone in the street is young and wearing red and face paint. Oddly, Valeria experiences a violent pre-match craving for cappuccino, which, for a phenomenal price, we obtain at an Italian-style café called Caffe Pascucci. The guy making the coffee wears a red Korea bandanna emblazoned with semi-mystical words in English: 'We are Twelfth'. Translation: 'We in our red millions, with our infinite zeal, with our fervour and noise, we are the twelfth member of the team. France has no chance.' By Italian standards, the cappuccino is a kindly disaster. The caffeine, though, will be handy. Outside the window, an apparently never-ending procession of gorgeous, kooky Koreans head towards the action.

By the time we get to Seoul City Hall Plaza it's about four hours before kick-off, and I was right: there's no space in the main square. But Valeria was right too: it doesn't matter a bit. At the centre of the immense crowd is a cluster of giant screens big enough to be seen from the surrounding streets, which is where we find ourselves, in a wide road near the Chosun Westin. We're about 200 metres from a stage and screen, but on a slope, so we have a perfect view over the immense, jigging throng. It's one of the most

astounding sights I've seen. I've known crowds of 100,000
and 200,000. This is bigger. As far as the eye can see, it's
a seething mass of red-devil lights, red shirts, happily
screaming faces, waving arms, plastic balloon sticks. And
the noise is extreme, partly because that's what happens
when two balloon sticks are smashed together rhythmically,
but also because a band on stage is whipping the multitude
into ecstasy. We stake a place on the edge of the crowd
and sit down, like everyone else, on the concrete. The
space behind us fills up rapidly. The band finish their set.
Soon the Australia–Brazil game is on the screens. The
Koreans want Australia to win because Australia's coach is
Guus Hiddink, hero and magician of Korea's success in
2002. But the relentless chanting is for Korea. Two main
anthems, through endless repetition, insinuate themselves
into a place somewhere between the gut and the soul. One
is a hypnotically repetitive chant, '*Deh-Han-Min-Guooh*'
(which means, simply, 'Republic of Korea'), and the other,
slightly closer to a proper song, goes, '*Ooooohh pitzey Co-
RAY-AAAAAH! Pitzey Co-Ray-AAAAAAH! Pitzey
Co-Ray-AAAAAAH! ORAY! ORAY! ORAY!* Hey! Hey!
Hey!' (meaning 'Victory Korea! Victory Korea! Victory
Korea! Ole! Ole! Ole! Hey! Hey! Hey!').

'football is software'

Seoul, 19 June 2006

Everyone around us – most in their teens or twenties – is warm and friendly. They offer us sushi and other food. Wherever I point my camera, people stop whatever they're doing, smile and give victory signs. Sadly, conversation is limited because our Korean is nonexistent and their English is poor. I go for a walk along the edge of the crowd and find the same atmosphere everywhere. Water-sellers and cushion-sellers and – what's this?! – dried-squid-sellers move in and out of the crowd. (Koreans are crazy for squid: they nibble the tentacles as we eat popcorn.) Near some fire engines and a grocery store (surely enjoying its best-ever night) I find a small gathering of clowns on stilts. On the way back, beside a tall fan with a colossal drum, which he beats incessantly, a sweet-natured guy called Tigger, named after the character in *Winnie-the-Pooh*, leaps up and down, gestures to the crowd and shouts, 'Time to get *crazy*!'

When I return I find that Valeria has bought a couple

South Korea–France

of inflatable cushions and made friends with two students who are explaining to her the similarities and differences between Korean and Chinese. Meanwhile, 200 metres away, in Munich, the Socceroos have failed in their attempt to take a point against Brazil. I suspect that the Koreans will survive their disappointment. I'm not sure I'll be able to say the same thing about my bottom. The concrete is hard and the cushion doesn't work too well; after a while it gives up and deflates completely. But – finally! – it's approaching four a.m. The chanting and balloon-stick-banging reach new levels of ear-splitting noise and people get to their feet. This is because 200 metres away, in Leipzig, the France and Korea teams have taken the field. Stupendous enthusiasm for the Korean anthem! The Marseillaise treated with considerable respect. And at last the game starts. In the first minutes there's more noise

South Korea–France.

than before! But – oh no! – after eight minutes France score a goal. I hope this doesn't make things too sad and bad round here. It doesn't. Indeed, at first, the French goal makes no difference at all to the singing, smiling, chanting and victory-sign-making. As the half progresses I realise it's damnably hard to follow the game in any detail. Inevitable in such a large crowd. In a stadium, even when things get rowdy, the architecture keeps the crowd focussed on the pitch. But in this tumult bodies and heads and stilts and armfuls of dried squid tentacles keep getting in the way. Many people in the crowd are simply chatting. Only the broadest essential points of the story (goals, sendings-off, dramatic saves) are getting through. Thierry Henry's goal inspires defiant singing (*'Pitzey Co-Ray-AAAAAAH!'*) but, however hard the crowd chant, let's face it, the Korean players in Leipzig are struggling. Yes, they still run around a lot. But the tactic no longer packs the same punch as it did four years ago: the Koreans conspicuously lack dash, *élan* or invention. I'm tired, but half-time brings a renewed burst of noise and optimism. New bands appear on stage and leaders of fan organisations visit our section, arms pumping. Patently wasted by now, most of the fans rouse themselves and stand and cheer again. I sit this one out but marvel as a Korean flag several metres wide passes from hand to hand above our heads. '*Deh-Han-Min-Guooh! Deh-Han-Min-Guooh! DEH-HAN-MIN-GUOOII!!*'

Meanwhile, something more fundamental even than sleep deprivation is changing the mood. The magic darkness of the night is giving way to grey dawn. In daylight, the sea of electrically lit devil horns looks less thrilling. When the game restarts, Korea play as badly as they did in the first half. A sense of helplessness is beginning to get to the crowd. About fifteen minutes from the end, Valeria and I stand up, say goodbye, offer condolences, suggest through

Seoul, 19 June. Seoul City Hall Plaza. South Korea equalise against France.

sympathetic gestures that it's no disgrace to lose to mighty France, and move slowly towards the subway station on the far side of the square. Trains will be running soon if they aren't already. Some other people are leaving. Now there are spaces in the crowd. Near the Plaza Hotel, opposite City Hall, a group of girls catch our attention. The faces of most of 'The Twelfth' have become despondent, but these girls remain utterly passionate and totally involved. Every move, every run, every misplaced pass in Leipzig causes almost unbearably intense reactions. The girls' faces reflect every emotion from feeble hope to pitiable anguish. Turning our backs on the screens, we focus on these amazing girls as they watch the dying stages of the lost match. Then a miracle occurs: the girls' faces burn with sudden, wild, improbable hope. The next instant they are screaming and leaping with incredulous joy. We spin around . . . Korea have scored! *What?! How?!* While the replays reveal the technicalities the square is going berserk. Noise like a jumbo jet taking off at close range. Fireworks erupt. Everyone is back on their feet, bouncing, hugging, yelling. A few minutes later the final whistle goes. The Koreans have got a draw.

Almost as soon as the match ends, the celebrations merge with the morning rush hour. Police move with military brusqueness to form a cordon allowing traffic to flow down the main road on the west of the square. After their epic football night most of the fans will go home, shower and go to work. Meanwhile, tens of thousands of others in suits and ties and dresses are heading for their offices. The euphoria of the fans is exhilarating, though. 'Again 2002' indeed. So the beatings of Italy, Spain and Portugal last time were no flukes? In the Italian manner, bikes and cars with flags zip by with horns hooting frantically. I'm wiped but, with Valeria's help, I undertake the silliest vox pop I've ever attempted. We stop passing fans, ask if they speak English, and if they say yes, try to interview them about what just happened. They all offer the same explanation: Korea achieved the draw because the French were an ageing team from an ageing country and Koreans are young and strong and brave and they never give up. OK, that's enough interviews. We've got to get home.

So what was last night about? What did it mean? The early evening after the morning before brings some theories to consider. The Korean media report that an estimated 700,000 young people spent the night on the streets in front of big-screen TVs. One newspaper suggests a sexual element to the Korean passion for football. After all, Korea is a controlled society and all-night football carnivals are a fine opportunity for young Koreans to be out together without drawing parental ire. A Korean Internet company claims a 300 per cent rise in condom sales during the tournament.

Valeria, meanwhile, has a bolder and more original idea. Like Colonel Kurtz in *Apocalypse Now*, she's been reading *The Golden Bough*, James Frazer's classic book about mythology and religion. She thinks that Frazer, writing in the 1890s, might explain the behaviour of Korean fans: 'Did you notice how in Rome nobody sang until the team scored? It was as if they had to wait for the team to give them a reason for singing. But the Koreans sang continuously all night, even when the team was losing. In fact, when they lost a goal they sang louder. Why do you think that was?' I don't know. 'Because the Koreans believe in sympathetic magic to influence events at a distance. They think the fortunes of the team depend on them. That's why they say "We are Twelfth". She shows me a passage which helps explain why the Korean fans try to forge a telepathic link between themselves and their team in Germany. Frazer writes that "belief in the sympathetic influence exerted on each other by persons or things at a distance is of the essence of magic. Whatever doubts science may entertain as to the possibility of action at a distance, magic has none; faith in telepathy is one of its first principles". He goes on to give lots of examples of tribes using this magic to try to help their warriors and hunters. Naturally, he never wrote about football. But is football not some modern equivalent of the ancient rituals of war and hunting? Some parallels between ancient tribes and young football-loving Koreans are striking. For example, among the Thompson Indians of British Columbia, "when the men were on the war-path, the women performed dances at frequent intervals . . . They painted their faces red and sang as they danced." And "when the men of the Yuki tribe in California were away fighting, the women at home did not sleep; they danced continually in a circle, chanting and waving leafy wands."

At six o'clock I have a date. I go underground to a fancy sushi restaurant two floors beneath one of Seoul's most prestigious office blocks. I've come to meet Dr Hongik

Chung, Professor of Cultural Policy at the Graduate School of Public Administration at Seoul National University and expert on football's role in Korean and wider culture. He'll set me straight.

I ask him what football means here now. 'The passion for football is quite new here,' he says. 'There is an outpouring of nationalism. Korea being a latecomer and trying to stake its place in the world, football just happened to be a good medium for that.' The catalyst was the unexpected success of Hiddink's team four years ago. Koreans found that football could project a potent image of the country to the world. 'We didn't expect success at all. Most of that was credited to Guus Hiddink, this unbelievable coach. Each win brought bigger cheering crowds on to the streets. It changed everything. It even changed the outcome of the presidential election.'

One irony is that, historically, Korean elites always looked down on sport. 'There's a story about one of the kings of the last dynasty who saw people playing, I think it was volleyball. He said: "It's fine, but why would anyone want to watch this?" That expresses our traditional attitude to sport: the idea was that it was OK but only as physical exercise. Here we are completely different to Japan, where the elite class was a warrior class, or to Europe where the ruling class was a warrior class. Korea wasn't like that. Here, the rulers were the literary classes. For thousands of years, they studied.'

The last World Cup changed attitudes, but crowds for the K-League are still small. This, though, will change. 'The K-League is not making any profit at the moment, but it is in the process of changing into a European style. In five or ten years, maybe, you'll see huge changes. At the moment Korean people are not so knowledgeable about football. But that is changing too. Young people have information about football in Europe. They know who are the good players.' They are connecting to the rest of the world, through the medium of football. But it will be on their own terms and with a distinctive Korean flavour. 'The world is getting smaller but at the same time, as they say, east is east and west is west. It doesn't mean that we become the same. Globalisation, getting closer and exchanging customs ideas and cultural stuff . . . It doesn't mean we become just like you.'

I float my idea about football as virtual TV-mediated experience. The professor agrees, but takes the notion further. 'In the future sports and all the other cultural industries will become huge, money-making businesses. In twenty years you'll see. It's the fastest-growing sector in the world; sport, movies, entertainment, education will change our traditional notion of industry. Manufacturing industries are being replaced by these software-type industries. And sport really is a prime example of a software industry.' I notice that the restaurant itself is a kind of theatre. As each customer arrives or leaves the staff roars out greetings and farewells in the Japanese manner. The professor's eyes twinkle, as if he's joking, but he emphasises the point: 'Football is software. It makes no physical material. It produces images for television, which of course is now the most important place for the consumption of sport. That is the future.'

psycho schoolgirls

Tokyo, 20 June 2006
Dortmund 3 p.m. – Togo 0 Switzerland 2
Hamburg 6 p.m. – Saudi Arabia 0 Ukraine 4
Stuttgart 9 p.m. – Spain 3 Tunisia 1
Berlin 4 p.m. – Ecuador 0 Germany 3
Hanover 4 p.m. – Costa Rica 1 Poland 2
Kaiserslautern 9 p.m. – Paraguay 2 Trinidad & Tobago 0
Cologne 9 p.m. – Sweden 2 England 2

The entrance to Tokyo is garlanded, but not in the way I expected. The train from Narita Airport swishes through the rice fields and bamboo and farmland and begins the long haul through limitless suburbs towards the heart of megalopolis. In the sprawling, tidy greyness of the city, every home is festooned with laundry. From low houses and apartment blocks alike, shirts and sheets and smalls wave and droop in the feeble breeze. Something seems to be missing, but it takes a while for me to work out what it is. Among the immense profusion of flapping fabric there isn't one blue shirt of the Japanese football team, not a single Japanese flag. After the red fervour of Seoul, it's clear that any passion the Japanese may have for their team, and for the World Cup, will take a different form.

It's been a lousy journey. The trip from Korea was meant to be a stress-free short hop. But my planning was awry. I'd figured that flying from Seoul (two hours and fifteen minutes) would be a breeze. I hadn't realised that we'd have to get up at six-thirty a.m. I didn't know we'd have to wait two hours at Narita (an hour for passport control, another hour waiting for the train). And I didn't know that the train journey itself would take another hour and a half. By the time we somehow find a way through the Shinjuku subway station (biggest in the world, apparently, and the most bewildering) and find a taxi and reach the New City Hotel we are totally knackered – again. Every time we get over one dose of jet lag we stay up all night to watch a match, or get up early to catch a plane . . . and promptly get a new dose of jet lag. I feel like Tom in *Tom and Jerry*: I'm trying hard, but my basic stupidity means I keep getting thumped by a smarter, more nimble opponent.

Compared to our spacious, light and comfy quarters in Seoul, the new hotel is expensive and bleak. The room is cramped and depressing, though it is possible to see the trees in Shinjuku Park if you jam your head right up against the window and crane to the right. We crash and sleep for a couple of hours.

I'd imagined I might be able to make some sense of Tokyo because I've seen a bunch of old Japanese art movies. The approach works OK with other cities. For instance, once you've seen *Wings of Desire* Berlin is a breeze. But no Japanese movie I've seen, not even *Godzilla Vs the Smog Monster*, prepares me for this place or helps me get my bearings. What's the point of Kurosawa and Mizoguchi when you're figuring out a subway system where each line is owned by a different company, where you have to buy different tickets for each bit of the journey and there's no one around who speaks English? How about Ozu's exquiste and moving exploration of family tensions in *Tokyo Story*? Utterly irrelevant. Even Nagisa Oshima's legendary *Ai No Corrida*, which is, after all, based on real events in Tokyo . . . Well, that's about a man and a woman who retreat from society into a world of sexual obsession and the movie ends with the woman strangling her lover and slicing off his penis. See what I mean? There is, though, one film that fits rather well with the average baffled Westerner's first impressions here – though it's not technically Japanese, having been made by Sofia Coppola. 'It's not fun, it's very, very different,' says Bill Murray of Tokyo in *Lost in Translation*. On our first night, without realising it or meaning to, we find ourselves all but acting out scenes from the film.

Our first urge is for food. We walk past the nearby Park Hyatt (the hotel in the movie) and find a terrific sushi place in the warren of gaudy, noisy, streets around Shinjuku station. It's like all the other sushi-on-conveyor-belt places I've been to, only better, fresher, cheaper. Three Italian lads with Roman accents come in and start ordering dishes with 'no wasabi'. After initial hellos, they and Valeria avoid conversation, as if embarrassed to have come all this way and found themselves so close to home. In Seoul, we were almost the only Westerners around.

Time to explore something. Shibuya, on the Yamanote Line, is recommended. At Shinjuku station we find someone to help us, then take the correct train (!) and, three stations south, emerge into an astounding visual hubbub: the massive

Tokyo, 20 June. Shibuya boy.

crowds and forest of neon at Shibuya station. It's a staggering place full of strange and beautiful people. Giant screens in every direction. Across from the station is the HMV store where the Scarlett Johansson character in *Lost in Translation* experiences a sense of weirdness and wonder when she sees dinosaurs walking across the face of the building. Just beneath that is a Starbucks with a perfect, high view of one of the wonders of Asia: the Shibuya Crossing. We find seats by the window, nurse coffees and juice and admire the setting. Technically, the Crossing is just four pedestrian walkways on a busy traffic junction. The colossal flows of people make it look more like a horizontal human waterfall. And what pedestrians! A self-consciously sexy funky hepcat crowd. One oddity is how many schoolgirls in uniform there are for this time of night. Then you realise they're rather old for schoolgirls. Their skirts and socks are high. They wear loads of make-up . . . And their demeanour is that of Gogo Yubari, the psychopathic schoolgirl assassin from *Kill Bill*. Then there are the Shibuya boys: slender, graceful and camp, their hair bleached, coloured and piled high in strange shapes. After a while you notice that they are cruising the crowds. Later, I learn that some of the girls dressed as schoolgirls are in fact schoolgirls. Some come to Shibuya to have sex with strangers in exchange for fashionable items such as Louis Vuitton handbags.

The streets behind and to the right of the Crossing are thronged with the outrageously dressed and beautiful, with fashionable shops, bars, cafés and video-game parlours. I think perhaps that if I ever grow up I'd like to become young and Japanese. I'm told there's a floodlit football pitch on the top of one of these buildings. A small cinema is showing the atrocious British hooligan movie *Green Street* (here it's called *Hooligans*). I still haven't seen too many Japan football shirts or national flags, though. Then, up a side street, we discover the Shibuya Football Tower, a five- or six-storey building which sells football merchandise and even footballers (some players have agents and offices here). The Tower, which curiously features a huge picture of the England team at the entrance, has just closed. Fortunately, its café-restaurant, called Estadio ('For Football Fans of the World') is open till late. Great! A perfect place to watch Germany–Ecuador. Because, frankly, I'm not going to want to get up tonight in the small hours to find a bar to watch

Trinidad–Paraguay or even England–Sweden (especially since England are already in the next round). At the entrance to Estadio is a notice proclaiming a worldwide brotherhood of fans and urging football-lovers to share the World Cup experience inside. As the bar's website, presumably written by a computer translation programme, explains:

Love the football the people who, exceeding nationality age and sex, it meets the place where, that ESTADIO. ESTADIO, as for that, the dining bar of the meaning, stadium. You adhered to the natural material, selected, you can gather the menu which is easy to the body from in the world, the place where information of the world regarding the football overflows.

Down the stairs, past the pictures of world-famous players and stadiums, Estadio turns out to be a big place and nice, though rather empty. The guy behind the bar explains that there's a cover charge of fifteen euros a head. Thirty euros to join the worldwide brotherhood? Let's try to find a cheaper form of international-football brotherhood. Down another street and up a hill, in a small park, a dozen young Shibuyistas away from crowds are dancing in semi-darkness. They are inventing a new form all on their own, a weird combination of martial-arts moves and hip-hop. We watch for a while, then go looking for another football pub. We find one! A sort of fusion-cuisine plus bar, which is showing the game in an unsual manner: projected on to a rough brick wall above the entrance to the kitchen. I'm the only one watching. In bas-relief eight time zones away Jürgen

Klinsmann prowls the touchline giving orders to his players.
Directly underneath him, and approximately the same size,
the Japanese chef reads a cookbook and gives orders to his
staff. Valeria pointedly reads her book. I sip lychee juice.
And in a galaxy far, far away, in sunlight, in Berlin, Germany
dismantle Ecuador with minimum fuss.

tokyo

21 June 2006
Gelsenkirchen 4 p.m. – Portugal 2 Mexico 1
Leipzig 4 p.m. – Iran 1 Angola 1
Frankfurt 9 p.m. – Netherlands 0 Argentina 0
Munich 9 p.m. – Ivory Coast 3 Serbia & Montenegro 2

It's Valeria's last day before going home to Italy and she wants to do touristy things rather than footbally things. I agree. There are no games during the day anyway. (Though I did catch Joe Cole's nice goal against Sweden. England will now avoid Germany in the next round, which is a shame because England–Germany makes the heart beat slightly faster than England–Ecuador.)

The shuttle bus from the hotel to Shinjuku station stopped running at ten a.m. We've missed that. So we splash out and take one of Tokyo's famous box-like taxis to the Imperial Palace. The white-gloved driver (all Tokyo taxi drivers wear white gloves) smiles effusively and offers us boiled sweets ('Japan Number One Candy!' he tells us proudly) as well as sticks of chewing gum. I've no idea why. The candy is indeed good, but the palace is off limits to commoners. We'll do what other tourists do: wander around the palace gardens. Before that, we buy sandwiches at a nearby café and meet an English banker who knows the city well. He tells me that I've got the wrong idea about the Japanese and the World Cup: 'They're completely obsessed with it. They talk of almost nothing else. Everyone I know is dog-tired at the moment because they stay up most of the night watching matches. They're puzzled as to why England are playing so badly. They ask me: "What's the matter with Lampard?" and "Why doesn't Gerrard play for England like he does for Liverpool?" They know all about everything.' I tell him about our time in Seoul, and wonder why the Japanese don't bother with similar displays of public enthusiasm. 'Oh, they would never do anything like that! It would be considered vulgar. With the Japanese, everything is much more internal, much harder to read. This really is a country like no other. I lived here for a number of years and I can't say I understand it even now. Most Westerners don't. We just don't get it and we never will. But there are about one per cent who come here and get completely hooked. They're the ones who never leave.'

The Imperial Palace gardens are splendid. Sandwiches, consumed atop the ruins of an ancient castle, satisfactory. We take in, briefly, a calligraphy exhibition and two beautiful and tranquil shrines near the Ochanomizu station. Yanaka, a low-rise, low-stress area full of temples and cemeteries, is the nicest bit, conveying some small sense of what the city must have been like before World War Two. The opulence of Ginza – like a bigger, neon-drenched version of New York's 5th Avenue – feels oppressive. And then Valeria gets mugged by a toilet. The Japanese are proud of their high-tech toilets. They regard them as evidence of their superior hygiene and technology. To outsiders, though, they can be terrifying. The basic concept is to combine the Western-style flushing toilet with an electronic bidet armed with an array of nozzles for spraying cold (or hot) water upwards. If that makes you nervous, be sure to never touch any button whose function you don't understand. Valeria makes that terrible mistake. It happens in the 'rest room' of a smart café near the new exhibition centre. She intended only to flush, but accidentally touched a button – and got blasted in the face by a powerful water jet from a cleaning nozzle. If it happened to Mr Bean it would be funny. Valeria considers it not funny. Don't let it happen to you.

tokyo

22–23 June 2006
Hamburg 4 p.m. – Czech Republic 0 Italy 2
Nuremberg 4 p.m. – Ghana 2 USA 1
Dortmund 9 p.m. Japan 1 Brazil 4
Stuttgart 9 p.m. – Croatia 2 Australia 2
Berlin 4 p.m. – Ukraine 1 Tunisia 0
Kaiserslautern 4 p.m. – Saudi Arabia 0 Spain 1
Hanover 9 p.m. – Switzerland 2 South Korea 0
Cologne 9 p.m. – Togo 0 France 2

Valeria must get to Narita early for her flight to London via Korea. In London, she'll rest with Daniele and then go back to Rome. We barely sleep all night. The last sight I have of her is her running off through the barrier. I already miss her terribly.

Back at the hotel, I try to sleep. Tonight it's Japan–Brazil at four a.m. I'm finding it hard to get excited. Japan have to beat Brazil by at least two goals to stay in the tournament. Fat chance. The *FT*'s man in Tokyo, David Pilling, advised me that the best place in the city to watch the game will probably be Nakata.Net Café, a fancy place in a fashionable district owned by (and named after) Hidetoshi Nakata, Japan's biggest football star, who used to play for Roma, Parma, Bologna and Fiorentina (and is currently on loan to Bolton).

I walk to Shinjuku, hoping to encounter some World

Cup fever. There isn't any. The subway is closed for the night and, compared to the usual demented bustle, the streets around the station are eerie ('It's quiet, Sarge . . . *too quiet*'). The only places open are a couple of bars, some love hotels and a McDonald's. This is a sleazy part of town, but it feels safe. I sit on some steps and observe. Like moving from sunlight into semi-darkness, it takes a while for the eyes to adjust. Then I begin to notice that, every now and then, small groups of young people in twos and threes, some wearing blue shirts, are quietly heading for places to watch the game. The same modest-scale migration is taking place in cars. There is football fever in the city after all . . . I just had to pay attention to appreciate it.

At this very moment, Hidetoshi Nakata must be in the bowels of the mighty Westfalen Stadium in Dortmund, preparing for the game. It's time for me to get over to his café in Omotesando and join the party. Until a few months ago, Nakata.Net Café was called something else and promoted the Sony Xbox 360 game console. Now it's the hippest World Cup-watching venue in Tokyo. Every game of the tournament is being shown live here. And, to make the atmosphere as international as possible, the management invites fans from countries involved in each match. I arrive at about two-thirty a.m. On the corner across the street bleary be-suited businessmen say solemn farewells to each other after a night of heavy drinking. Outside the café, blue-shirted fans are queuing. The café is already nearly full. The majority of the couple of hundred inside are young women. Most wear the blue of Japan. Not all have Nakata's name on their shirts. Near the main door is a little group of Brazil fans, most of them also Japanese. Even more confusingly, there's a Western woman on her own wearing an Australia shirt and clutching two little plastic Australian flags. Of course. I'd all but forgotten. At four a.m. Australia also play Croatia. Assuming that Brazil will beat Japan, Australia only need a draw to reach the next round. Go on, Guus.

The large room is bright and has a high ceiling like a school hall. At one end, above a busy bar, is a cinema-sized screen for Japan. Smaller screens will show Australia–Croatia. There's a section of raised seating facing the big screen and more seats on the far side. In the middle is the main standing area for the Japan fans. I'm directed towards an area on the left marked 'Press'. I know why I'm here (I think), but why do other journalists think it interesting to watch people watching TV? At three a.m. the press corps arrives *en masse*. There are at least five TV crews, lights, microphones, a bunch of photographers, radio and newspaper reporters. In fact there are almost as many journalists to watch the fans as there are fans to watch the game. Journalists start interviewing each other. I join in by interviewing a nice reporter from the Kyodo News Agency. He claims to speak English but this turns out to be not completely true. So I do both parts. First I ask a question. Then he looks unsure. I suggest an answer, and he agrees by nodding. Later, when I play back the tape, the only voice I can hear is mine, and all my questions and answers are rubbish.

The atmosphere is part carnival, part circus, and it's getting noisier by the minute. Favourite chants involve the word *Nippon* (Japan) in various combinations with itself, such as: '*Nippon!* [clap clap clap] *Nippon!* [clap clap clap] *Nippon!*' or 'Wooo! Wooo! *Nipppooooonn! Niiiippon Niiippon Niiippon!*' The hardest-core fans are near the front. Some wear samurai masks. I work my way to the front and raise my camera. The samurai guys throw themselves in to a variety of fierce victory poses. Then they insist on taking pictures of me with them. One notices my red Korea bracelet, tied to my camera strap, and gives me a blue Japanese bracelet, which he assures me is much better.

As kick-off approaches, there's a personal message to the fans – from Nakata himself! He has sent us an email. His words appear on screen and are read aloud (to tumultuous acclaim) in Japanese and English.

Our goal and our task are clear, and, for this reason, I don't have any doubts or feel any need to panic about the upcoming match. My mind, too, is perfectly clear: 'Give all I've got in order to defeat Brazil.' [Wild cheering] We need to beat Brazil by at least two goals . . . There is no point in worrying about preventing our opponents from scoring unless we score ourselves. So I'm hoping to make this into the kind of match where, rather than winning 1–0, we might even lose 3–4. [Cheering and applause] We have nothing to lose except our pride. And that's what we have to protect. For all the people who have played parts in my life up until now, and for all those who believe in me now, right until the very end, I am going to fight this fight to the last moment, with all I am!! [Wild applause]

The café answers with devout chanting ('*Nakata! Nakata! Nakata! Nakata!*'), but Nakata cannot hear us.

Finally TV takes us back to Dortmund. On the main screen, with loud sound and commentary, the teams wait in the tunnel, where Nakata chats amiably with Ronaldo. On the small screens Australians and Croats get no sound. All four sets of players come on to the pitches. Australians and Croats are forgotten. The Japanese anthem is sung deafeningly. The little crowd of Japanese Brazilians at the back do a very decent version of the Brazilian anthem too. Whistles, incredible, high-pitched cheering and chanting and . . . we're off! The acoustics of the hall and shape of the ceiling amplify the noise, making this quite simply the loudest football-watching experience of my entire life. Whenever Japan cross the halfway line, kick the ball out of play or make a tackle, the noise becomes deafening. When the Japanese goalkeeper makes a save, it's even louder. Japan shoot hopelessly from long range and the ball drifts harmlessly into the crowd behind the goal . . . and the café roof nearly bloody lifts off. Actually this isn't fun. It's getting painful. I improvise a pair of earplugs, plunging tissue paper into a glass of beer and stuffing the wet tissues in my ears. Ahhh. Bliss! Now I don't care even if Japan score – which, obviously, they won't. Japan promptly score. The café goes crazy, but in a muffled way. On replay, the most interesting thing about the goal is how badly Brazil defended. Come to think of it, the World Champions are playing like beach donkeys. If the score stays like this till half-time this game could get interesting. Oh. Just before half-time Nakata's friend Ronaldo equalises. Silence from

Tokyo, 23 June. Japan–Brazil.

the blue shirts. Noise from the yellow ones.

In the second half, as revitalised Brazil play with some aggression and easily score three more goals, the mood in the café changes. The noise decreases (except among the Brazilian contingent). Blue-shirted girls watch with increasing levels of anxiety, pain and dejection etched across their upturned faces. Their hands are clasped in prayer or twist in supplication. Long before the end, the game has become a one-sided bore.

Meanwhile, almost unnoticed, a genuine epic is unfolding. It's hard to focus on Australia–Croatia when almost everyone is still boisterously keen on Japan–Brazil, so I've missed important bits of the story. The basics I've grasped: Croatia scored early; Australia got a penalty late in the first half (I went across to point it out to the Australian girl). Things got compelling a few minutes ago when Croatia scored again thanks to a goalkeeping mistake (but not by Schwarzer – who's the Australian goalkeeper?). Anyway, now Australia have to score again. Which is a tall order. It's getting late, late . . . The faces in the crowd in the stadium display deep emotion. The teams, evenly matched, are playing like lions. Harry Kewell, the Australian winger once described by the *Guardian*'s Richard Williams as having 'a heart the size of a diamond ear stud' is inspirational. He's almost playing the Croats on his own and . . . *Ohmygod!* . . . He *scores!* Amazing! What a game! Now all hell breaks loose. Every time I look at the screen the referee is sending someone off. First, it's a Croat. Then an Australian. Then another Croat gets a second yellow card. Then another Croat gets a red. Four sendings-off in one game? And all in the last fifteen minutes? It's a record and it's totally absurd. (I find out only later that English referee Graham Poll in fact gave one Croatian player three yellow cards and sent him off *after* the game. Still a record, but a different record.)

By six a.m. the Socceroos are through. Guus Hiddink, Harry Kewell, the entire population of Australia (and those of the UK, the Netherlands and South Korea as well, probably), and me, and the Australian girl (who I now know is called Anna Berry) are buzzed . . . And all the Japanese in the room (including the Brazilian ones) know none of this because they're still busy with the movie *Brazil 4, Japan 1*. It ends with humiliation for Japan. On the big screen Nakata lies flat on his back in the centre-circle in tears. In the hall, the Japanese Brazilians, who surprisingly turn out to be genuine Japanese Brazilians, from Brazil, who speak Portuguese and everything, dance and chant and wave yellow flags with unseemly braggadocio. A small number of blue-shirts slump to the floor and cry.

The café empties. Through the door, it's faintly shocking

to see daylight. I'm jet-lagged again. It's too early for breakfast, but Anna and I go looking for breakfast anyway. A Starbucks (they're everywhere) is opening, but won't let us in. We can come back 'in seventeen minutes' if we like. We don't like. Down the road a McDonald's (they're even more everywhere) is open. It seems pitifully banal to eat an Egg McMuffin in the middle of one of Tokyo's funkiest and most fashionable districts, but what else can we do? Anna Berry turns out to be smart, funny and quite possibly the coolest person I've met on my entire journey. She's one of that one per cent of native English speakers who comes to Japan and never leaves. She's been here five years, speaks and writes perfect Japanese and does about a million other things as well: public relations, translating, NGO work, UNESCO work, a degree in linguistics. She's only twenty-six but has already been twice around the world, once as a dancer, on a boat.

nuclear-free zone

Vancouver, 24 June 2006
Second Round
Munich 5 p.m. – Germany 2 Sweden 0
Leipzig 9 p.m. – Argentina 2 Mexico 1 (after extra time)

I'm even more tired than usual because I couldn't bear the thought of not watching Korea–Switzerland (at four a.m.). Foolish, but I had to know how the Korean story would end (or not end). So I sat up, toying (in a *Golden Bough* magic way) with the plastic red bracelet until the Swiss scored their second goal just after dawn. I felt a pang for the multitudes in Seoul, then I crashed. At least France made it, though.

On the way to the airport I reflect on the nature of Japanese World Cup TV advertising. In every other country so far (except in Britain when the BBC shows a game), TV coverage comes swaddled in a suffocating blanket of football-related puff. Some commercials are better-made than others, but, as a rule, the TV audience everywhere is assumed to be so obsessed with the game that any and every product under the sun (banks, insurance, beer, cars, credit cards, etc.) can and must be yoked to football and national fervour. The phenomenon is so ubiquitous that, like gravity, you stop thinking about it . . . Until you see the half-time commercials on Japanese TV. Alongside the usual bouncing balls and actors pretending to be more excited about football than life itself, their ads feature other sports: sumo, golf, even ice dancing. Flipping through the channels, I was also stunned to discover that 'the Johnny Carson of Japan' (the bottle-blond, pink-suited nutter who interviews Bill Murray in *Lost in Translation*) is real. Or rather, that the TV show in the movie is based on a real show, in which the non-Johnny plays the same character. His name is Takashi Fujii, his show persona is Matthew Minami. At three in the morning he was busy being his trademark loud, camp, silly self, humiliating a pretty girl by making her wear ridiculous pairs of glasses, and, well – actually, he's really rather good. A star performer in any language. I wish I understood Japanese.

I thought I would love hearing English again, but I don't. Settling in for the Air Canada flight across the Pacific, conversations around me feel like an assault on the deepest parts of my brain. Why are you all talking so *loud*? I don't want to *hear* about your hiking, your garden, your car. Leave me *alone*! Let me *think*! The stewardesses seem big and bossy. It's all because I'm tired. News on the screens concerns ice hockey and baseball. Another freakishly short airline night. I manage to doze a total of about five minutes. After 'breakfast' comes . . . mountains! I wasn't expecting mountains. And they're not European, Alp-like mountains, either, which take only a few minutes to cross. These mountains are fucking huge, and they don't stop: jagged peaks and snow and rock marching to the horizon, hundreds and hundreds of kilometres of mountains. We're getting lower and lower . . . A breathtaking view of Vancouver. We descend. We turn slowly. We get an extraordinary, clear view of one of the most beautiful cities in the world. As we step on to the tarmac I realise why the team for which Ruud Krol played in 1980 was (and still is) the Vancouver Whitecaps: the city is ringed with beautiful white-capped mountains. Somewhere back there we crossed the dateline. Which means that this time lurch is more brutal than the last one. I've gone backwards. I left Tokyo late on Friday afternoon. The flight lasted eight and a half hours. Now it's Friday lunchtime. Work that out. My body can't.

Vancouver is the first stop on the way to Buenos Aires (to see Argentina in the quarter final). I'd never realised how far away is Argentina. The flying time there from Tokyo is almost twice that from London to Sydney, and more awkward. There are no direct flights. I must go through North America, stopping first on the West Coast, then going on via Washington, DC. I could do it all in one thirty-six-hour stretch but, as I'm already fatigued, that would not be a smart move.

The original plan was to go through Los Angeles. I'd hoped to see a friend from Rome, a former girlfriend, an English movie legend (with whom I'd wanted to watch England–Germany) and a porn star. (That's four different people by the way). But Chase, from Rome, won't be there. Annie is pregnant, can't travel and wants me to fly instead to San Francisco (but I can't face more flights). There's been no word from the film legend (take that as a no). And porn star Tatum Reed didn't answer my last email, so the prospect of meeting her is iffy at best. I'm sad about that because I expected her to be one of the stars of my journey. We're not exactly friends, but we do have an email acquaintance dating back to Berlin last November. I was browsing Craig's List for apartments and found a great place near the old Berlin Wall. The advert described the premises, amenities and price and then, at the bottom of the page, it linked to the landlady's website, www.ilovepopwhore.com. If Jean-Luc Godard had been a revolutionary postmodernist porno artist rather than revolutionary Maoist film-maker, he might have had a site like Tatum Reed's. Her graphic trailers of multifarious sex with men and women were full of jump cuts, arresting music (composed by her) and daft slogans such as 'I am the Future of Entertainment' and 'Welcome to the Leisure Class'. The website also revealed that Tatum was in the process of writing a postmodern novel ('Imagine *Catcher in the Rye* remixed with *Shopaholic*, *Patriot Games*, and *Penthouse Forum*') and was a political pundit for the right (no details given). Thanks to Google, I further learned that she was a former professional ballet dancer who had a difficult relationship with her parents, and that her grandfather was an auto-industry bigwig in Detroit. I'd emailed her saying that I couldn't afford the apartment but would love to interview her for an English newspaper, maybe at World Cup time. Her story had a Berlin angle and I wanted to depict her as a kind of one-person combination of both

Christopher Isherwood and his friend Sally Bowles. (Isherwood was the writer; Sally, played by Liza Minnelli in *Cabaret*, was the 'woman of scandal' who inspired his *Berlin Stories* and whose identity he refused for decades to reveal.) Tatum liked the idea but now lives in California rather than Germany. Nothing materialised. Not then, nor (despite several emails) since.

Anyway, now I won't be seeing Tatum or anyone else in California. Instead, I've come to Vancouver to stay with my cousins. After Korea and Japan, I'm hoping for a blessed few days of calm. It would be nice to see some football too.

Somewhere over the north Pacific (just south of Alaska, I think) Germany made easy work of beating Sweden. After I clear passports and customs there's still time to catch most of Mexico–Argentina in a Brit-style pub in the arrivals hall, surrounded by various Canadians, Mexicans, Brits, Portuguese and other travellers. I had worried that Vancouver would be a World Cup desert, but there are almost as many people in football shirts here as there were in London; more than in Rome or Berlin (though both cities must be a bit more lively shirts-wise by now). After yen and won and złotys, Canadian money is immensely comforting because it features portraits of the Queen. I'm not tired; I'm exhausted. But the game is great. If Mexico win, I don't have to go to Argentina. I can make do with Brazil instead. Then Maxi Rodriguez scores a goal of maxi beauty and sends Argentina through. I'm going to Buenos Aires as planned.

The first thing everyone told me about Vancouver was how beautiful it is. Everyone was understating. Even from the back seat of a taxi on the way to cousin Alan's house in the western suburbs this is obviously true. The place sparkles. After the demented bustle and anti-pollution face masks of Tokyo, Vancouver seems almost comically tranquil. On the radio, the big news of the day is a local demonstration for world peace. (Jihadis please note.) Signs announce: 'Vancouver Nuclear-Free Zone'. True, the taxi driver reveals a faint hint of a dark side by chuckling over a murder story involving a lovers' tiff which turned violent, the twist being that the couple were in their late eighties. But it's a very old case and from somewhere else. It's hard to believe anyone in Vancouver ever even thinks of murdering anyone. How could they? They must spend their entire lives in a daze, stunned by the cleanliness and the water and mountains and forests all around. In sports news, the German and Argentina victories are the second item, behind transfer speculation concerning Vancouver's ice-hockey team.

My cousins are the nicest, kindest and sweetest people in Canada. When I arrive, one of the first things I see is a photograph of myself aged two weeks with my dad. It's lovely and I've never seen it before. It was taken by Alan's wife, Inga, in those days a professional photographer and dead ringer for Audrey Hepburn. Alan was – still is – an illustrious civil engineer. When they moved to Vancouver he helped build much of the city. Now he lives in the ground-floor apartment of his dentist son Andy's amazing house. From the terrace and upper floors there's a tree-punctuated view of the Burrard Inlet, the Lion's Gate Bridge and bits of the city. Behind the house, homes rise to a pine-covered ridge. Beyond that, nothing for hundreds of kilometres except mountains, trees, rivers, lakes, tundra and ice. We're on the edge of the wilderness. There is no human habitation between here and the North Pole.

The family let me sleep for a few hours, then take me for dinner at a delightful fish restaurant. After that Andy and Alan drive me to a high place and show me the entire city. It's chilly, dark and clear. Everything shimmers and sparkles. The great city sparkles, especially downtown. The great ships waiting in the Inlet sparkle. The planes gliding gracefully on the approach to the airport sparkle. I've never been so tired, but this may be the loveliest cityscape I've seen.

vancouver

25 June 2006
Second Round
Stuttgart 5 p.m. – England 1 Ecuador 0
Nuremberg 9 p.m. – Portugal 1 Netherlands 0

Just before David Beckham scores for England against Ecuador I tell Alan: 'David Beckham's going to score.' There's nothing particularly impressive or interesting about this prediction, as there is almost nothing impressive or interesting about the game as a whole (or indeed about the England captain at the moment). It's a question of probabilities. Beckhambauer (as I now think of him) is overdue a free-kick goal against someone. The kick is in a perfect position on the edge of the box. There's a good thirty per cent possibility of the ball going into the net.

Later in the day, though, comes a moment that's less easy to account for. In the fifth minute of Holland–Portugal the TV director gives us a close-up of Giovanni van Bronckhorst and I see him being sent off, which doesn't actually happen until about eighty minutes later. Strange. My clairvoyance doesn't extend to anything else in the match. I fail to foresee the other three red or sixteen yellow cards. And, right until the final whistle, I keep thinking that Holland are about to rescue themselves with an equaliser and go on to win. About Holland's exit . . . Well, what can one usefully say? It upsets me. But talking about the game in normal terms seems as pointless as trying to review the first night of a play interrupted by a flamethrower-wielding maniac who burns down the set and maims the actors. Referee Valentin Ivanov's performance is staggeringly inept ('Valentin's Day Massacre', someone in England later calls it). He loses control completely. But Portugal's relentless fouling, diving and cheating is worse. Holland were not without fault (think of Boulahrouz's foul on Ronaldo) and the Dutch finishing was poor. But that's not why they lost.

Vancouver, 25 June. After Holland–Portugal.

Anyway, now I'm too miserable to even think about football. In the hot lunchtime sunshine we leave the air-conditioned pub on Marine Drive and head off in my hired car to North Vancouver to see Inga. Stricken with MS, she lives in a care home surrounded by pine woods. Alan spends as much time with her as possible, but he can no longer drive because of what he calls his 'immaculate conception' – the macular degeneration of his eyes. Inga gets around in a little electric buggy and tires easily. She makes me forget about Holland and Portugal. Later, Alan gives me a tour of some of Vancouver's most beautiful places, which are truly spectacular.

vancouver

26–28 June 2006
Second Round
Kaiserslautern 5 p.m. – Italy 1 Australia 0
Cologne 9 p.m. – Switzerland 0 Ukraine 0 (after extra time)
Dortmund 5 p.m. – Brazil 3 Ghana 0
Hanover 9 p.m. – Spain 1 France 3

In other sports it is expected that cheats will be heavily punished. Ben Johnson, for example, cheated by using banned drugs in his preparations for the 1988 Olympics. In the 100-metre final his behaviour was exemplary and he won in world-record time. But a drug test established his earlier crime and he was punished. In horse-racing, riders who gain unfair advantages over their rivals are disqualified. Yet in football cheating works. It works just fine.

Today's exciting Australia–Italy match turns putrid at the end when Fabio Grosso dives in the penalty area over Australian defender Lucas Neill. It's an artful deception. Grosso's leg jerks backwards, as if tripped. The referee awards a penalty. Totti scores from the penalty. Italy thus win a match they looked likely to lose. Australia go into shock and out of the World Cup. But, within seconds of the penalty decision, TV replays establish pretty conclusively that the referee was conned. Neill did not move. Grosso flicked his own leg back at the vital moment. The cameras, in other words, have caught Grosso cheating just as the drug test caught Ben Johnson. Johnson was stripped of his gold medal and has suffered a lifetime of disgrace. But will there be retribution or sanction of any kind for Grosso's deception? Of course not.

Among Anglos the idea that fairness and good sportsman-ship are important in sport still runs deep. In Italy (and else-where) a different philosophy prevails. As Gianni Brera said, in Italy the concept of fair play does not exist. Anything to obtain an advantage is legitimate. The key thing is to not get caught. I watched the match with Alan's granddaughter, Michaela, a talented fifteen-year-old footballer who plays for the province of British Columbia and was picked for Canada's national team in her age group last year. She can certainly play a bit. Yesterday she scored a goal direct from a corner. She is shocked by today's outcome. 'I wanted Italy to win,' she says, 'but not like *that*.' From Rome, by contrast, comes an email from Valeria. People there are celebrating vividly and dancing in the streets. The son of one of her madder neighbours (a woman who celebrates every Roma goal by standing on on her sixth-floor balcony shrieking for several minutes and waving a Roma flag) appears on the balcony wearing only his underwear . . . and shrieking and waving a Roma flag. Meanwhile, from Tokyo, Anna Berry emails in a more Australian state of mind: 'I know referees are only human, but this guy's judgement was way out! The red card [for Materazzi] should have been yellow, but particularly the PK [penalty kick] that wasn't even a foul!!'

And me? I'm upset and depressed. In fact I can't remember the last time I felt so angry about something in football. At the same time I suspect I might be being a touch precious and unreasonable. After all, have I not happily accepted dodgy penalties as part and parcel of the game when they're for my team? Well, yes. And Grosso is hardly the only cheat in this World Cup, is he? Everyone's at it (though not the Germans): diving, pretending to be hurt, deceitfully winning throw-ins, free kicks, corners and penalties; wasting time; tricking the referee into giving yellow and red cards to opponents. Furthermore, a certain level of injustice is integral to the game. We accept that referees and linesmen fail to see all that the camera sees and make mistakes. In some ways we relish injustice. A sense of grievance — often lasting decades — is an essential element of every club and country's football narrative. In England we enjoy the righteous indignation that comes with memories of being cheated by Maradona in '86. The Dutch cling to the legend of Holzenbein's *schwalbe*. The Germans enjoy telling and retelling the story of Geoff Hurst's goal that never crossed the line . . . And so on. We tell ourselves that what goes around comes around. These things balance out in the end . . .

Except that none of this convinces me this time. I'm appalled that Grosso got away with it. His offence is a prime example of cheating so widespread that it corrodes the essence of the game. Football works like fiction. Just as there are rituals and conventions to be observed in story-telling (the rituals and conventions which allow an audience to enter a fictional world), so a football audience has to be able to trust the essential rituals of football. If the game becomes fundamentally dishonest it will die. Which means that diving, cheating and other forms of gamesmanship are eating away the essential fabric of football. Unfortunately, it's too late to book Grosso, award a free kick to Australia and restart the game at 0–0 with thirty minutes of extra time to play (which would be fair). But something will have to be done to stop cheating. Video evidence must be used. All forms of cheating and gamesmanship must be punished, retrospectively if necessary. Cheating will have to be treated as harshly as violent conduct.

On the other hand, even a bit of cheating would have enlivened the terrible Switzerland–Ukraine game. Who cared who won? Not me. The match was made bearable only by watching from a pub overlooking English Bay Beach. France–Spain, on the other hand, was fantastic (apart from a dive by Henry). The spectacle of France's old men suddenly playing like angels was immensely moving. The supposedly extinguished talents of Vieira and Zidane suddenly flared up like bombed oil wells. You may think you remember me saying something earlier about Spain winning the World Cup, but I'm sure I didn't. I think you'll find that what I actually said was that France would win the World Cup. Glad to get that sorted out . . .

lightning without thunder

Vancouver/Washington, DC, 28–29 June 2006

I say my goodbyes to Alan and Andy and Sue and the sweetness of Canada and it's time to go east and south. This will be by far the longest journey of the trip. For once I'm early. I don't stop anywhere to admire the views. I drive straight to the airport. I go to check-in – and discover that there's been heavy rain around Washington and my United Airlines flight is delayed by four hours. *Four hours?!* Allowing for the time difference, it means I can't get to Dulles until one a.m. at the earliest. Which means I have no chance of making the connecting flight, which leaves at nine-forty-eight p.m. Which means I'll now have an unwanted twenty-four hours in Washington, DC. Which means that, if I'm lucky (i.e., the plane tomorrow evening isn't delayed as well), I'll get to Buenos Aires with two hours to spare before Argentina's quarter final against Germany. Which isn't quite what I'd dreamed of. But what can I do? Something bad was bound to happen at some point on the journey. I've been lucky that things have gone mostly to plan so far. Is there anyone from United I can talk to? 'Only at the check-in desk, sir.'

The queue for the check-in desk takes an hour. There's a nice Korean guy behind me in the same boat (or plane) and with an even longer journey ahead. He has to get to Natal in northern Brazil, which involves changing in São Paulo. He will miss his connecting flight too. Finally I reach the check-in desk and ask about my options. What if my Argentina flight has left Dulles by the time we arrive? Is there space on the next flight? Where can I stay if I'm stranded in Washington? I have nothing to worry about, says the check-in guy. At worst, I'll be on tomorrow night's flight. And because my connecting flight (this one) is delayed by mechanical problems, which are United's responsibility, United will put me in a hotel in Washington if I need one. Anyway, there's a chance that tonight's Buenos Aires flight might also be delayed so I might even make that. I'll just have to go to Dulles and take it from there. I ask: 'You're sure about the hotel? I really don't want to spend the night in the airport.'

'Absolutely. The plane was late arriving in Vancouver; the delay is our fault, so you will definitely get a hotel room.' On the plane the pilot makes a further announcement. He apologises for the delay, which he explains was partly due to severe thunderstorms and heavy rain around Washington, and partly to mechanical problems.

They weren't kidding about the weather. On the way to the east coast we are treated to a light show as we fly above not one thunderstorm but a whole flotilla of thunderstorms. I've never seen lightning from above before. It's not the way it looks from the ground. It's not a case of seeing one or two flashes and waiting for a bang. From inside the plane you hear no bangs. But there are continuous, colossal flashes of lightning across whole chunks of sky, only slightly obscured by the clouds which generate them. Is it safe to fly through this stuff? By the time we start our descent the sky has calmed. We land without incident.

An announcement: my plane to Buenos Aires (and planes to other destinations, too) left a couple of hours ago. I ask a stewardess where I need to go to find out what happens next. She tells me to be patient. Staff at the United desk at a nearby gate will help me. There's no one at the desk. Someone will be coming shortly. Refugees from earlier flights are all around, spread out on the floor or slumped in chairs. Dulles is a charmless airport at the best of times, and it pretty much closes down by midnight. Apart from us, the only signs of life are the cleaning staff, who clean noisily, the bright neon lights and the continuous tannoy announcements. Sleeping here would be almost impossible. The passengers disembark. The captain and crew leave. Finally someone appears at the help desk. About twenty of us have missed connections and need assistance. The first piece of news is good: I am booked on to tomorrow night's flight to Buenos Aires. The second piece of news is not good. United cannot offer any of us places in hotels because hotels in the area are very busy and anyway the delay to the flight was caused by bad weather and not mechanical problems of any kind. Quite frankly where we spend the night is not United's responsibility. That's

Joo on Pennsylvania Avenue. 28 June.

outrageous! Yet even before I launch into protests ('But in Vancouver I was promised . . .' 'And the check-in guy said this . . .' 'And on the plane the pilot said that . . .') I know I am wasting my breath. The desk staff say their lines without any trace of embarrassment. They seem practised in this sort of behaviour. I discover later that United has one of the worst reputations in the business.

There is a silver lining, though. Joo, the Korean guy, and I are already allies. Now we meet a wiry English student called David. David doesn't need to get to Argentina or Brazil. He only needs to get across town to his digs at College Park in Maryland. The journey by taxi would take about an hour at this time of night, but, as a student, he can't afford a taxi. Well, if we share the cost of the taxi, would David have space on his floor for us to sleep? He would indeed. Saved! As it turns out, several of David's room-mates are away, so Joo and I both end up with a bed for the night. For which we will always be grateful. David turns out to be a smashing bloke too. And prodigiously smart, doing a PhD in mathematics. I deeply admire his kind of thinking because it's so far above and beyond anything I can manage. For example, David specialises in partial differential equations, numerical analysis, fluid mechanics and nonlinear elasticity. Are you with me so far? Nor am I. But in the morning David patiently explains what his thesis is about. If I understood him aright, it's about predicting how liquids behave inside tubes or cylinders. A nineteenth-century Frenchman defined the problem and it's a classic in mathematics. But now David has introduced a new element: what if the cylinder isn't smooth but is irregularly shaped? What happens to the liquids then? More to the point, how can mathematics describe and predict what happens? Yikes! I give up. But David does not give up. I get the feeling he'll solve this problem and add in a small but significant way to the sum of human wisdom. By strange fate, then, the contemptible behaviour of United Airlines has allowed us, albeit briefly and imperfectly, to enter a higher world of thought. Who'd have thought a missed flight could broaden the mind?

palermo viejo, buenos aires

30 June 2006
Quarter Finals
Berlin 5 p.m. – Germany 1 Argentina 1
(After extra time. Germany win on penalties)
Hamburg 9 p.m. – Italy 3 Ukraine 0

> 'What vernacular and violent fates were being acted out
> a few paces from me, in the smoky bar or in the dangerous
> wasteland? What was that Palermo like or how beautiful
> would it have been if it had been like that?'
>
> Jorge Luis Borges

Amid the heat, humidity and stress of midsummer
Washington, Joo and I spent the afternoon near the FBI
building. He went sightseeing on the Mall (I've seen it). I
tried to write in a bookshop café. At the airport, United
shafted Joo some more. When we arrived last night, they
assured him that no United Airlines flights would be leaving
Dulles today for São Paulo. No planes at all. No, sir; not
even full ones. So Joo would just have to fly all the way
down to Buenos Aires with me, change planes, fly back to
São Paulo, change planes again and try somehow to find a
connecting flight on to Natal . . . All in one stretch. That's
probably going to take him two extra two days if he's lucky.

As we wait to board at Dulles, a tannoy announcement:
'Would the last remaining passengers please proceed

immediately to gate such-and-such where United Airlines flight so-and-so to São Paulo is about to depart.' To São Paulo? This airline is without shame! I might have thumped someone at that point, but Joo swallows his anger, remains his lovely warm, reserved self. The flight to Argentina is uneventful, except for some turbulence over Bolivia. I even manage to sleep almost half an hour. At touchdown, we hug our goodbyes. Now I have to get into the city quickly because Germany–Argentina starts in about an hour and a half. In my book, Argentina should win this. But at passport control the officer offers a sign that people here are nervous. 'Against the Germans. It's local for them. It could be complicated.'

I've never been here before. Never even been in South America before. Everything is brand new. New city. New light. New colours. New trees. New horses. New hemisphere. New climate. New language. But at least I'm still in more or less the same time zone as just now. Compared to my last seven countries this is pretty cool (in temperature) and grey and poor. Argentina may have recovered well from its economic meltdown five years ago, but most cars on the way in from the airport are jalopies. Some have whole sections of bodywork missing or held together with string. There are many Peugeot 204s. Pale-blue-and-white flags everywhere, draped from shoulders and balconies, from windows, taxi aerials. Countless people are wearing the national-team shirt that is like no other. I wish I could have been here yesterday to savour the build-up. Mind you, the celebrations when Argentina win will be fantastic. On the radio, a local station is having fun by telephoning

London bookmakers and asking about odds on today's game. The announcer speaks to a succession of baffled staff. Argentina are slight favourites.

I have just enough time to check in at Malabia House in the Palermo district – nice hotel! – and shower before I need to hurry to see the match. Eric, the reception guy, makes two suggestions. There's a sports bar, which will probably be full and is over *that* way. Alternatively, *that* way lie cafés and bars. Well, that's easy. I'll go that way. I'm light-headed from lack of sleep and food but walking fast down the street called Honduras. Low buildings, cobbles, trees with dead leaves. Hurrying people. Noise. Colour. Well, just one colour actually: pale blue. I reach a corner and a locked glass door. The place is called Café Malasartes, meaning 'Café Evil Arts'. People inside are watching the football. I try the handle. A young woman with large, pale-blue eyes and long black curls appears on the other side of the glass. I speak loudly so she will hear me. I explain: 'I am an English journalist. I am travelling around the world to watch the World Cup and I have just flown all the way from Japan to watch this match here . . . with you.' Pause. She unlocks the door and gestures me inside and points to the only free chair in a room thick with simple wooden furniture, families, food and smoke. The redbrick walls are hung with paintings. Steel shutters block out the light. She picks up something from the counter – a pale-blue-and-white scarf – hands it to me and says: 'Maybe you'd like to wear this.' Through an arch is a huge TV screen, and from the semi-darkness, thunderously, from the game just under way in Berlin: '*Deutschland, Deutschland* . . .'

It never occurred to me until recently that it might be worth the effort to cultivate an appreciation of Argentina. This must go back to childhood. In England in the late 1960s it was a name one didn't hear much. I remember something about a tall man in stripes who wouldn't leave when sent off in football. There were children's-book words like 'pampas' and 'gaucho'. But I wasn't even quite sure it was a real place. Argentina or 'The Argentine'? Argentinians or Argentines? No one seemed to know. By the time I became adult, other words had introduced themselves: *junta*, *desaparecidos*. There was a popular song, too, about not crying, but I never saw that show. Argentina was still visible mainly through its football, and its football seemed almost mythically lawless and remote.

The next two hours in Café Malasartes suffice to blow all that away. The next two hours in Café Malasartes suffice to make me fall in love.

It's an osmotic thing. How can you be in a room full of people in the grip of deep passions, primal joys and fears without beginning to share their emotions? You can't. It's basic human psychology, football's equivalent of the Stockholm Syndrome whereby hijack victims come to share their captors' point of view. It has already happened to me in Poland and Korea (though, strangely enough, not in Stockholm). Around me is the most passionate crowd I've encountered on the journey. This is no fiesta (at least not until Argentina win). Dress is modest. No one here has felt the need to dress up in unduly elaborate costumes or apply comical face paint. There's no hysteria or drunkenness or malice. Just complete identification with the unfolding drama. Young and old, the beautifully expressive faces turned towards the screen are like those of children utterly absorbed by a film or magic show – which, of course, is exactly what this is.

In Berlin, the first half is mostly cagey, though Argentina display more of the stuff needed to win football matches. In the bar, each pass, run, free kick or surge in either direction evokes a symphony of oooohs, aaaahhs, scrunched faces, wide eyes, nervous movements of hand, head and body. Two middle-aged women are tearing paper (napkins, newspaper) and putting the pieces into a wicker basket. It's a bit previous, but they're making confetti, to be flung when Argentina score a goal.

At half-time, a girl with an orange headband, a student, makes a point of coming over to talk. She tells me that this is usually a quiet Bohemian place and she often comes here to study. Why the orange headband? Is it for Holland? 'No, no. It's just a nice colour. It's my way of saying I like football, but I don't like nationalism.' We turn to the match. This, she believes, is the game that will decide everything. How so? 'If we win this game it will be all done. We go at least to the final. Then we see from there. We know we can beat Italy or Ukraine. We don't worry about Brazil. But this is Germany and we are scared. This is the match, the huge match.'

Right at the start of the second half, things turn Argentina's way. The blue shirts have been outplaying the white ones. The TV sound is way up. An Argentina corner swings in from the right. In the one and a half seconds it takes for the ball to reach the penalty area, the voice of the commentator begins to soar. As Ayala moves, the crowd sense it too. By the time the ball has been transferred, via Ayala's head, to the net, everyone is on their feet screaming, punching the air, crying, whooping, knocking over furniture, hugging and jumping up and down. The commentator's trademark scream of 'GOOOOOOOOOOOOOOL!!!!' goes on for about forty-five seconds before he draws breath. Then: '*ARRRR-gg-entina UUUNO! Alemaña . . . ZERO!*'

Malasartes is now covered with confetti. And now everything begins to go wrong. Does fear from the café somehow communicate itself to and freeze the players? Or do the players panic the supporters? From my position in the little wooden chair it's hard to tell. Either way, within a few minutes of the goal, game and mood have changed. Instead of imposing themselves and finishing off Germany, as they must, Argentina fall back and try to defend the lead as if they were Italians. But they are not Italians. (Not even if this district, Palermo, was once the Italian quarter and many of the Argentina players are of Italian descent.)

Coach José Pekerman takes off his conductor Riquelme and brings on defensive midfielder Cambiasso. This doesn't help. The Germans hardly need to be invited to attack and now lay siege. Around me, the mood shifts in a few minutes from worry to alarm to the distilled essence of terror. The people around me are arguing furiously about Pekerman's tactics. 'No, no, no,' moans a man with the saddest brownest eyes. I change my position to better watch the crowd. There's a woman in black I hadn't noticed before whose face reflects anxiety in it. purest form. When the Germans

Buenos Aires, 25 June. Argentina–Germany.

get close enough to shoot, she hides her face in her hands. When Argentina clear their lines, or their goalkeeper makes a save, or a shot passes harmlessly, she stands up and shrieks with relief. She uses a kind of voodoo, twisting her hands into the Sign of the Devil (thumb and middle fingers curled inwards, index and little fingers out) and makes nervy stabbing movements at the screen, trying to hex the Germans, but the Germans keep coming. Ten minutes from time, Germany score. The collective sigh from Malasartes is like the last breath escaping from the lungs of a hanged man.

The worst thing imaginable having now happened, the team and the bar crowd relax slightly. The team begins to play with more freedom, as if a burden has lifted and the match reverts to the pattern from before the goals. But the damage has been done. There ... a feeling that Argentina have missed their chance. When penalties arrive the mood is grimly pessimistic. The girl with the orange headband is too nervous to speak. It all goes badly. I've been wearing my scarf for two hours now. I'm upset too. Cambiasso's final miss is greeted with anguished cries. I notice that in Berlin fighting has broken out between players. Here, most people just sit and stare. A mother and father comfort their small son. A few rueful smiles. I look around for the woman in black, but she's left. I don't know what to say to the girl in the orange headband, who has a faraway look and tears in her eyes. So I say: 'I'm so sorry.' She says, 'Me too,' and gives me a hug.

What happens next? I'm barely aware. After the game the adrenaline fades and leaves me stranded. I go back to the hotel, carefully fold my scarf, which I now treasure, carefully lay it over back of the chair and fall asleep. Now it's dark. I go for something to eat. A noisy restaurant in a nearby street named after Jorge Luis Borges, who grew up here. I visit a lovely bookshop on the corner of two other streets. This beautiful district (less crowded with fashionable bars and boutiques in his day) greatly influenced Borges. Consider this, from one of his biographers, Edwin Williamson:

Although by the time the Borges settled there, the neighborhood had calmed down somewhat, Palermo still carried a colourful legacy of cabarets and brothels, a place where violent men and lusty women danced the tango and told stories aflame with gauchos, knife fights, and vengeance. It was a legacy that . . . cast its spell over much of Borges' earliest work.

The lusty women, cabarets, colour and 'spell' bits are still around. Didn't see any knife-fights, brothels or gauchos. *Mañana*, maybe.

buenos aires

1 July 2006
Quarter Finals
Gelsenkirchen 5 p.m. – England 0 Portugal 0.
(after extra time. Portugal win on penalties)
Frankfurt 9 p.m. – Brazil 0 France 1

One a.m. I finally get the wireless Internet working. It doesn't work in my room, however, so I sit in the lobby/lounge, which is nicer. It's a really cool hotel. Comfy, nice, stylish, friendly . . . I send emails for the first time in forty-eight hours. I even managed to edit and upload photographs from the game yesterday. Such emotion in those faces! Now I'm just dog tired. Dog. Dog. Dog. But I can't get to sleep. I don't know what time it is. Can't sleep, clan't cleep. All I want is sleep. Only sleep. Let me sleep. Please. Sleep. Sleep. Just . . . I wake up. I must have slept. The room is dark. I fumble for my mobile phone, which hasn't worked as a phone in the last five countries, but still works OK as a watch and alarm clock. Eleven a.m. This means . . . What does it mean? Wait – Six a.m. Vancouver time. Nine a.m. Washington time. Tokyo . . . Oh-who-cares. Must be two o'clock in Britain, three o'clock in Germany (or is it four in Germany and one in the UK?) No . . . Hang on. Start again. Wait. If it's eleven here – and it must be, because I remember resetting at the airport – that means . . . Oh, wow – it means an hour before England–Portugal kicks off. Which means I can take a few more precious moments in bed . . . Yeah, that's all I want just a few more minutes and I'll . . .

Fall asleep.

In my dream I wake about twenty minutes into England–Portugal, just in time to see David Seaman (thought he'd retired?) concede a really stupid goal. First he saves it, then he lets the ball trickle under his body very slowly at the near post. I knew he should have never come back. That's what they say: 'Never go back'. And why are these people in my bedroom? They're watching the game. Actually it's more of a pub than a bedroom. There are five big TVs on the wall, all showing the game. Oh no: another goal for Portugal, but the picture is so fuzzy and there are so many people around I can't see what's happening. I don't mind about the people until someone vomits in the fireplace. Now I get really angry and tell everyone to leave. I'm waiting at the bus stop because I've got to get to the game. I've got to get to the game . . . Got to get to the game. Wake up agai . . .

Oh no. Oh bugger. I missed the game.

Malabia House calls itself a 'design' bed and breakfast. But the light switch is so far from the bed I'd actually have to move ten centimetres to the left and raise my arm to turn the light on. What kind of design is that? If I were the designer I'd have fixed it so a person could wake and turn on the light without physically moving. OK. Try to

find the remote instead   Find the remote, press a button.
The room floods with TV light (not sunlight, thank God).
On TV a bunch of England fans are hanging around inside
the stadium after the game. I wonder why they aren't
leaving. Maybe it's half-time? I summon Captain Oates-
style courage and reach all the way over to the other side
of the big bed to check my watch. It's still fifteen minutes
before the game! I haven't missed a thing. These pictures
are just a different style of TV. They don't do interviews
and panels. They use cameras in the stadium to do what
you actually do when go to a game: they get there a bit
early and hang around waiting. Wish our TV did that. I
sit up and get unexpectedly emotional at the sight of English
people far away in my bedroom. They look pretty silly,
some of them. Lots of red and white. Lots of large bellies,
too, but these bellies are nice. Ordinary bellies, not hooligan
bellies like it used to be. Bellies like these it's a pleasure
to see. World Cup '66 shirts. T-shirts. St George crosses
everywhere. One man has a polar bear on his head. His
wife or girlfriend has huge, huge tits, wears a tiny, tiny St
George-flag bikini. My people!

Two and a half hours later I wish I had missed the game.
I had remained in bed for the first half, then had a quick
shower and went looking for something to eat. This is an
amazing hotel! Because most of the people who stay here
are either vampires or go dancing all night, the hotel does
never-ending breakfast. Someone offers me full breakfast,
then brings it to me in the lounge, and three of the guys
who work here watch the rest of the match with me. The
breakfast (eggs, toast, fruit salad, yoghurt, cheese), the guys,

and even the furniture in the lounge are all much more impressive than England's performance. For most of the game I wonder why Gerrard isn't playing. Then I realise he *is* playing. Pablo reckons Wayne Rooney is a crazy man and thoroughly deserves to be sent off. I suggest an alternative explanation: Rooney was just a little upset and confused (which can happen to anyone, can't it?) and obviously didn't realise that Carvalho was on the ground and therefore stamped on Carvalho's groin by accident. I phone Dad in London. His view is somewhere between mine and Pablo's. What really exasperates him is Sven's earlier tactic of using Rooney as lone striker. We completely agree that England's missing of three penalties was a scandal. Dad sums up the mood of the nation: 'I don't think anyone minds too much because the team's been so bloody terrible all the way through.' There's much anger, though, towards Cristiano Ronaldo and the Portuguese for their by-now routine diving, gamesmanship, etc. Apparently Ronaldo ran fifty metres to the referee to demand Rooney be sent off . . . and then winked triumphantly at the Portugal bench when Rooney was sent off. Argentina TV didn't show that bit.

It'll be Brazil–France in an hour. Back in the lounge, Pablo tells me a story. 'You know what happened this morning? I got a phone call from Brazil. The guy says: "This is very important. I need eleven rooms urgently for tomorrow night. Do you have eleven rooms?" I say, "Well, I'm sorry, sir, but we don't have that many rooms. We are almost fully booked." And he's laughing and he says: "Yeah, yeah, but you don't understand. I need *eleven* rooms

. . . for the Argentina team because they're coming home early from the World Cup! Ha ha ha!" And I can hear his friend laughing, and he's laughing, and then he hangs up. You have no idea what it's like living next to these people. It's like that all the time with them. "Brazil this, Brazil that . . . Oh we're so great . . . Don't you know how *great* we are?" They never stop. Never! If they win the World Cup again I can't stand it. They have five stars already. It's too many, too many! Six stars would be . . . Oh you can't imagine anything that bad.'

The nice Brazilian restaurant I noticed last night on Costa Rica street might be a good place to watch France–Brazil. But Ma Leva Brasil turns out to be completely packed with yellow shirts. People are standing three or four deep on the pavement, all straining to see in through the window. I'm not sure I want to do that, especially as I'm not really on their side. I want France to win. With Holland and England out (along with Australia, Argentina, Spain, Poland, Trinidad and South Korea) I've got to support someone. Why France? Two reasons, both of them beginning with an A.

The boring reason is that Thierry Henry, Patrick Vieira and Sylvain Wiltord play or used to play for my team, Arsenal. The second reason is Zidane. Great players are always compelling, like great actors are always compelling. But his story has suddenly taken on extra, mythic resonance. All of a sudden, Zizou resembles King Arthur (that's the other A). To be more precise, he resembles King Arthur in the last part of the story, after the ruin of his kingdom, after the forces of evil have laid waste to all his dreams and hopes, the ageing king who must lead his ageing knights into redemptive battle for one last time. I must confess that Zidane has never grabbed me this way before. I liked him in 1998 (but it wasn't love), then I stopped liking him in about 2000 (can't remember why), then I admired him without exactly loving him for a few years, then I rather forgot about him. But now I'm besotted, entranced, enthralled. I also discover I like him as a personality and character: brave, decent, gracious warrior – all the attributes of the classic hero. Better yet, he's the hero who returns. We thought he was a shadow of his old glory, and then he plays that extraordinary game against Spain. It was as if some magic had lifted a curse. Everything he was, he is again. But here's the kicker: it can't last because he's dying. To switch stories, Zidane is also the replicant leader at the end of *Blade Runner*. His life (read career), designed to be cruelly short, now has only an unspecified number of minutes to run. It could finish in the next ninety minutes, or the next, or the next . . . Whatever happens, it's 'time to die'. With all that going on, how could anyone possibly not want France to win?

The overflow from Ma Leva Brasil is across the street in the larger Bar Janio. The first half is mesmerising and tense. And . . . Have you ever seen anyone playing better than Zidane is now? Brazil are supposed to be a great team but he's dominating them. Just embarrassing them. Stronger, wiser, more accomplished than everyone else, and he inspires the other old Frenchmen. Shame they haven't scored yet. Second half: more of the same. France had better get a goal soon or my King Arthur stuff is going to sound stupid. All the Brazilians in the bar are quiet now. And – *Yaayy!!* – France score! A French/Argentinian couple called Audrey and Carlos are at the table behind me. About ten minutes after the goal they start softly singing the Marseillaise. It's not quite Victor Laszlo singing the Marseillaise, but it makes the hairs on the back of the neck stand and I'm moved to join in for a couple of lines, which is my limit as I don't know all the words. I tell Audrey and Carlos about my journey and its purpose. Carlos recalls a moment from yesterday. Being one of the very few people in the city not glued to the game, he took a number 132 bus to Once. The streets were largely deserted and the only other passenger was a young woman who was listening to the match on the radio, through earphones. Carlos says: 'I knew Germany had scored because the woman took off the earphones, looked out of the window and there were tears in her eyes.'

The game is over. France made it comfortably in the end, though right in the last moments the Brazilians briefly began to sing and sway and hope when Ronaldinho had a free kick. Later, in Recoleta, near a Subte (subway) station, I encounter a tall grey-haired man walking the streets very slowly with a tight smile and waving a tiny plastic French tricolour. I tell him the French team was magnificent. He says: 'And tonight I am the only Frenchman in Buenos Aires.'

buenos aires

Enjoying France's win is all very well but now look at me: totally stranded on the wrong side of the world, 8,000 miles from where I need to be, which is France, Portugal, Italy or Germany. Who'd have thought that for the first time in seven World Cups neither Argentina nor Brazil would be in the semi-final? Not me, obviously. I got it completely wrong. So, too, did the British bookies who were offering short odds on an all-South American final. I feel like the coach who picks his form players, deploys his most reliable formation and then sees everything fall apart in the last few minutes of the match. That'll teach me to go round telling people the joy of football is its unpredictability.

I'm not the only one here having trouble facing the new reality. No one in Buenos Aires wants to take down their blue-and-white flags yet, or even take off their blue-and-white shirts. In a restaurant last night, still decorated with flags and blue-and-white balloons, a cheesy-looking TV documentary about the Argentina victory of 1986 was showing with the sound off. The title was something like *Twenty Years of Glory* and the film featured long interviews with the second-rank stars (no Maradona or Valdano) and freeze-frame slow-mo replays of Argentina's most important goals. I know this mentality, this escape into nostalgia. It's what we do in England. Perhaps the Brazilians are having problems coping with their exit too. Who'd have thought it? South America is suddenly as relevant to the World Cup as Kathmandu and the Faeroe Islands.

I need to get back to Europe as quickly as possible. But I can't. I've spent most of the day on the Skype phone trying to change my ticket. In London I was promised this would be a cinch. Now I discover it's the opposite. My next scheduled flight is with Lufthansa tomorrow, to São Paulo. But I don't want to go to São Paulo any more. I want to go to somewhere in Europe (Berlin or Rome, preferably) for the semi-final. I need to call Lufthansa. But Lufthansa in Buenos Aires is closed. I phone Lufthansa in London. Hold on for twenty minutes. Get through. Get cut off. Try again. Same thing. Call Lufthansa in Germany. Lufthansa in Germany tell me to call Lufthansa in London. I finally talk to someone in Lufthansa in London, who tells me that Lufthansa can't actually change anything. The only airline that can change my ticket is Asiana Airlines, because my first flight was with them. Which means that technically they issued the ticket. But there is no Asiana office in Buenos Aires. I call Asiana in Korea. Asiana in Korea tell me to call Asiana in Los Angeles . . . To cut a long story slightly shorter it seems I can't change my ticket because it's a paper ticket. The only way to change it is to send my old ticket to Los Angeles by FedEx and get them to FedEx me the new one. OK, let's explore that. Where can I go to? Ummm . . . He'll call me back. He calls me back. And the answer now is . . . I can go – nowhere. All flights from Buenos Aires must go through São Paulo, where there is no possibility of a quick change – I'll have to stay over for twenty-four hours. And there are no flights of any kind back to Europe from São Paulo for another two weeks, except the flight on which I was originally booked on Thursday. In other words, I have to stick to my original route. Damn. The only alternative would be to buy a new ticket to Rome or Frankfurt or London or Paris but on another airline. That would cost about the same amount of money I paid for the round-the-world ticket, which I can't afford. Bugger, bugger, bugger.

What choice do I have? I'll stick with the original Thursday flight (to London via Lisbon) but I don't see any point going to São Paulo tomorrow now (the original plan). I'll stay here for another two days, because I like it. It's a glorious place, and who knows when I'll get the chance to come back? I've fallen for the cafés, the faces, the archi-tecture, the shops, the mood, the weather, the people, the language and even the buses. At this stage I don't think I could bear to take on yet another new city in yet another new country, especially when there's no point. So I'll try to relax. Be cool like Fonzie about the whole fucking thing. I'll go to São Paulo early Wednesday afternoon, catch most of France–Portugal (though I'll miss the start) at the airport. I'll go to a hotel near the airport. I'll sleep. I'll fly to Europe on Thursday. It's a hideous journey but at least it's the last. If Portugal beat France, I'll stay in Portugal and watch the final there. If France win, I'll be back in London by Friday morning so I can get to Berlin or Paris or Rome on Saturday or even (if I'm really exhausted) on Sunday.

Meanwhile, it's Germany–Italy coming up. Strange. After weeks of frenzy, suddenly there are hardly any games any more. It hits me that almost all the previous games didn't matter. Poles, Ecuadoreans and me apart, who now gives a damn about Poland–Ecuador? An email from Árpad is headed 'See You in Berlin!' He reckons that Germany will beat Italy and reach the final. He is confident that I'll fulfil my promise and watch it in Berlin with him. I'd love to. Berlin is transformed. As to Friday's game, already receding into distant history, he feels sorry for Argentina, a place he loves. Mainly, though, he is amazed by the change in Germany. Millions celebrated the penalty win with an impromptu carnival. The best news comes at the end. It has nothing to do with football but does involve pictures on a screen. The screen of an ultrasound machine: 'I saw our lovely daughter! For the first time on a big screen, alive and kicking! She is so sweet.'

Pablo Salomón, film-producer friend of a friend from London, invites me to his place to see Italy–Germany. He's warm, smart, funny, generous and good company. A colleague, a film director called Alejandro Israel, will be there too. They need to discuss a new project (a film version of Euripides' *Iphigenia in Tauris* relocated to a remote region of Argentina), but, in the event, football takes over. As

Circus Maximus, Rome. (picture: Alessia Piovanello)

Germany and Italy warm up, Pablo puts on an Argentina shirt decorated with a Rolling Stones logo and poses by the TV for a picture. 'It should be us! We should have been there!' He takes off the shirt. Then Marina, his secretary, arrives and does a similar ritual with the same shirt, though she flaps it in front of the screen. 'We really should have been there. This should be us!' Point made, we all settle down. We would all quite like Germany to win. Alejandro arrives. He's for Italy. Turns out to be one of the best matches of the tournament, marvellously tense. It is settled (or so it seems to me) by Germany's brilliance at penalties. After seeing what happened to Argentina, Italy, desperate to avoid a shoot-out, attack desperately. Right at the end Grosso scores the decisive goal. It's perfectly brilliant, and his emotional celebration rekindles sweet memories of Tardelli '82. On the other hand, I can't help thinking that Grosso was also the guy who cheated Australia. By the time Del Piero delivers the *coup de grâce* the whole building is rumbling in celebration. Many Argentinians have Italian roots and for the next hour and a half phone lines to Italy are jammed. About two hours after the game I get through to Valeria, who watched with her best friends at Circo Massimo, the Circus Maximus, a location approximately thirty minutes' walk from my flat, or ten minutes by bus, or five minutes by car. What, I ask myself, was the point of spending thousands of euros, flying 30,000 miles and experiencing ten types of jet lag to watch silly Japan–Brazil when the biggest Italian event in a decade is taking place on my doorstep? Rome has gone nuts. Even now it will take Valeria an hour by foot to reach her car. She is surrounded by shouting, whooping, hooting fans on Via Appia. She's saying things like 'Incredible! Amazing! Fantastic!' I say: 'I thought you didn't like football.' She says: 'I don't like football. But I do like being with all the people. It's a party, a carnival! Come back soon. You should be here!'

são paulo

I have my last breakfast at Malabia. I'll miss it and the whole city, which I've spent a little too much time running around. I have a sad taxi ride to the airport. In exchange for some of my last pesos I permit a man in a uniform to wrap my suitcase in blue clingfilm. Not quite sure why I said yes to that. Looking out the window of the aeroplane at the big country below I find myself humming the Talking Heads song. 'I'm tired of looking out the windows of the airplane/I'm tired of travelling, I want to be somewhere . . .' The plane is late, so I've missed most of Portugal–France. There are TVs showing the match everywhere, even in baggage reclaim. At least France are winning. There's the penalty again. Thierry's exaggerated dive is a species of mime, but the guy did take his legs. King Arthur puts it away beautifully. As Mark Fruin would say: 'Is Zidane the dog's bollocks or *what*?' Thanks to history and shared Portuguese language (which seems to consist entirely of the sound 'ssshhhhzzzzzzzssshhhzzzzz' but is perfectly understandable when written down) the Brazilians want Portugal to win. But the Portuguese are rank ordinary and some of their diving is so preposterous as to be funny. Thank goodness they're out. I definitely won't stay in Lisbon tomorrow, then. Never seen the point of third-place games. Rome here I belatedly, tiredly come.

The shuttle to the Ibis Hotel, Guarulhos, takes an hour to arrive, converting a fifteen-minute journey into an hour-and-fifteen-minutes journey. I'm deeply tired. The hotel is far from great. It would have been nice to finally meet Marvio from the *Folha*, São Paulo's newspaper. We've interviewed each other and spoken often, but he can't make it out here tonight. And it would take me an hour each way in a taxi. Next time. Guarulhos is apparently famous for its metallurgical works but the main business in town seems to be hotels. An economy based on journeys delayed, missed and interrupted. Over deeply mediocre food I try to make sense of a lavishly produced soap opera and chat to a philosophical engineer, who is en route to Peru. From my room on the tenth floor Guarulhos is not as nice as Buenos Aires. Below I can see the backs of people in the throes of religious rapture through the windows of an evangelical church. Ten metres from the church is an 'American bar'; it has a gaudy red-neon sign and appears to be a brothel. To the right, two prostitutes stand under a street lamp waiting for passing cars. I sleep. I wake several times in the night. By the morning I have a sore throat and feel vaguely ill in a flu-ish sort of way. By the time I reach the airport, there's no mistaking it. I have a fever. Whatever I do, however bad I feel, I have to make that plane.

lisbon/london

6–7 July 2006
Rest day

The queue at the check-in takes an hour. The TAP flight to Lisbon is torturous and lasts almost forever. The big Austrian with intrusive elbows in the next seat makes sleep impossible. I try to be distracted by the in-flight movies, one concerning a mermaid who needs to sleep in a water tower and likes shopping and is in love with . . . someone or other. Later, there's news. Portugal have lost to France; a women's group seems to be expressing concern over spousal abuse after the match; a story about Cristiano Ronaldo's girlfriends. By Lisbon I'm feeling worse. Waiting for the flight on to Heathrow I find myself in conversation with the member of a team of Brazilian evangelists travelling on to Guinea Bissau. He speaks American English but his fervour is Brazilian. His theory (widely shared, according to the engineer last night) is that Brazil's defeat by France must have been the result of a conspiracy: 'No one knows the real story, but that was not the real Brazil. No way!

Something happened to make them play like that.' Right. No strength left to argue. I get three seats to myself for the last two hours back to Heathrow, and sleep. When we land, almost the first person I see is Bob Geldof, heading to Africa, maybe, perhaps to save it from Brazilian evangelist conspiracy theorists. The corridors are womblike and carpeted. The next person I see is an old friend currently living in Rome I haven't seen in over a year. 'That's *amazing*!' she says 'I was *just* thinking about you! I had a feeling I was going to meet someone who would be able to help me. Can you lend me £10?' I hand over the £10, decline coffee and promise to see her in Rome in the next few days.

By the time I reach my parents' house by taxi, I'm desperate for sleep, coughing and running a fever. I dose myself with aspirins; collapse in bed. The adrenaline that carried me here is now spent. The cumulative exhaustion of the last weeks runs me over like a train. Can I get to Rome? I can't even think about it until tomorrow. I sleep for hours . . . Wake feverish . . . Sweat . . . Drink . . . Take aspirins . . . Dream . . . Sweat . . . Sleep . . .

london

8 July 2006
Third-place match
Stuttgart 9 p.m. – Germany 3 Portugal 1

The fever is higher. There's no way I can get to Rome in this state. Dad suggests going to Lille instead, by Eurostar train, but I barely have the energy to get up and down the stairs. I call Valeria and tell her I'm not coming. She takes it badly. Much later, I drag myself downstairs for the third-place game. Nice to see Germany win in style, amusing to hear the German crowd boo the now-notorious Ronaldo every time he gets the ball.

london/rome

9 July 2006
Final
Berlin 8 p.m. – Italy 1 France 1
(After extra time. Italy win on penalties)

My temperature reads 102. I feel defeated. Árpad emails to say he'll be cheering for Italy: 'I will turn into a *tifoso* now, Italy being closer to my heart I hate and love Italy at the same time.' From Valeria something more anguished: 'We're going to Circo Massimo three hours before the game hoping to find a comfy place to sit, possibly on the bank of the circus. The weather is not promising. Huge clouds are threatening Rome. Supermarkets are empty. We tried to buy some panini to take with us but it seems everybody had the same idea. The migration of Romans towards the centre started in the early morning. I'm so upset that we can't share this. You were supposed to be here today. What was the point of coming to Korea if we can't do this together? I don't understand how life works.'

Nor do I. Maybe it's like this. The World Cup is a metaphor for life. We try to live our lives and plan our

round-the-world World Cup journeys rather as a coach
tries to run a team. He can scheme and plot a possible
route to the final, he can pick the best players, he can even
make them practise penalties . . . but ultimately Fate will
decide the matter. Going into the World Cup, the only
sure thing is that almost everyone will lose at some point.
There are thirty-two teams. Only one can win; everyone
else goes home sad. OK, so I'll be with those guys. Mum
chips in with a cheery thought: 'Won't it completely ruin
your book if you're not in Rome for the final?' I've been
wondering about that too. 'Yeah, probably. But only if
you think my journey needs a triumphant happy ending.
Maybe a downbeat, tragic ending is better? Maybe it makes
me interesting?' Dad says: 'It's hardly a tragedy. You went
all the way round the world and realised that the best place
to watch the final was with your old dad.' Mum settles the
point with a decisive flourish: 'Would you like a nice cup
of tea?'

Just before I actually, physically turn into Dorothy at
the end of *Wizard of Oz*, Valeria and I speak and decide
to implement a desperate Plan B, a journalistic equivalent
of the third-place match. Since I cannot be at Circo
Massimo in person, she will impersonate me in every
detail. She will observe, take notes, cough, speak terrible
Italian, scratch her beard, etc. And we'll speak at regular
intervals through this night of nights. The idea is: that I
will experience virtually her virtual experience of the
match in Berlin.

Half an hour before the game, Gary Lineker floors me
completely by launching into his own carefully prepared

metaphor about the World Cup as story. Lineker is seen posing beside a statue in Berlin depicting books and writers. He surveys the story of the World Cup so far. Has it been a thriller? A tragedy? A whodunnit? Most importantly, on final night, how will the story end? He's expecting a twist. I'm really impressed. I thought my theory was original; maybe it's just a statement of the obvious.

Meanwhile, Valeria has arrived in the Circo to join its biggest, noisiest crowd in 2,000 years. The BBC also has a reporter there, though it's hard to see anything from his pictures except that there's a big crowd waving flags. My reporter is better. Valeria and friends have a great spot in the middle of the crowd, near the biggest screen. Valeria is enthralled. 'The Italians are the *best fans in the world*,' she enthuses. 'They're so original and funny and warm. They're not organised and sophisticated or stylish, like in Korea, but we are much more individualistic. More fantasy.' The atmosphere is *festa* rather than semi-religious rite and, instead of buying commercial T-shirts, most *tifosi* have home-made costumes. Valeria is wearing white trainers, white tights, a green dress, red top, Neapolitan lucky-charm necklace – and red/white/green face paint. Her friends Alessia and Mariasole have face paint too. Alessia's boyfriend Andrea wears a black T-shirt with the picture of a Milan fan from an 80s trash movie and the word '*Viuuuulenza*' ('violence').

The prize for best headgear would surely go to a man who's made a precarious-looking half-metre hairnet out of red, white and green plastic cups. Another man, dressed as a Roman centurion, is running up and down the centre of the Circo waving a stick. The banners, too, amuse. One says. '*Non c'avete manco il bidé*', Roman dialect which translates roughly as: 'You [the French] haven't even got bidets'. Another declares '*Io I Galli me lo mangi*', which is apparently funny because it's a pun – *Galli* meaning both Gauls *and* chickens. Geddit? 'I eat Gauls/Chickens.' Ermm . . . doesn't make me laugh, but then I'm not Roman and I'm not even there. It's hot and dusty and Valeria reckons the crowd is bigger than the one in Seoul, though it behaves differently. The Romans don't believe in telepathic magic. It's not their job to help the team in Berlin. It's their job to have a good time. Before the match there are lot of songs, especially endless repetition of the first seven notes of the brilliant White Stripes song 'Seven Nation Army', a Roma chant which is now Italy's World Cup anthem. But, once the game is under way, the spectators tend to . . . *spectate* until something exciting happens on the field. King Arthur's penalty brings stunned dismay, Materazzi's equaliser riotous jubilation. Through the second half and most of extra time the crowd grows increasingly quiet. Back in London, Dad and I want France to win: we worry in the first half, grow increasingly confident in the second and during extra time . . . Until – talk about a *twist* in the tale! King Arthur suddenly turns into a completely different and darker character. Macbeth, perhaps? No, no: too much planning. Hannibal Lecter? Oh no, no, no – that doesn't work at all. Or maybe – yes, here's the perfect fit – Barry Lyndon in the scene where he loses his temper, beats up his stepson in front of all the guests and destroys his reputation for ever. *C'est*

Rome, 9 July. Valeria at Circus Maximus.
(picture: Alessia Piovanello)

incroyable/è incredibile! Zidane has become a Stanley Kubrick character.

In the Circo, the headbutt brings shock which turns rapidly – as Zidane gets sent off – to wild celebration. As we all struggle to take it in, it strikes me that Zidane has done something exceedingly rare in fiction. He has changed category, pirouetting effortlessly from being one great archetype to being another. One moment he is a hero. The next he is a tragic *flawed* hero and, thereby, much more compelling. I decide to identify madly with Zidane. He has been let down at the last moment by some hidden inner flaw. I have been let down at the last moment by some hidden inner flaw. The headbutt decides the match and will be the only thing about the game – or even the entire World Cup – that anyone remembers or talks about.

When penalties come, no one in Rome expects Italy to win. In London we don't see how France can win. Fabio (I haven't forgotten even if everyone else has) Grosso scores a perfect winning kick. In the crowd of half a million, everyone is suddenly jumping on top of everyone else, screaming, dancing, hugging kissing and waving flags. Then there's water flying everywhere. Valeria gets soaked to the skin. The Comune di Roma provided thousands of free water bottles – why waste them by drinking? Over the next hours, the whole city turns out to shout, sing, greet total strangers as long-lost relatives, stand on top of buses yelling and wave flags. After several hours of walking and partying, Valeria and the girls reach the car and get home happily exhausted.

The next day, the Italian team returns to Rome with the trophy for a triumph any emperor would have envied. Again, the focal point is the Circo but Valeria decides to sit this one out. We share the experience by phone on more equal terms, as British TV also shows the pictures. When the team arrives in the Circo, Alessandro Del Piero takes off his shirt and bellows to the crowd while team-mates face silly questions from compere Carlo Verdone. ('How did you feel when you saw your wife after the game?' 'Well, I was really happy to see her.') The ceremony packs a surprising emotional wallop. The size of the crowd and the sheer magnitude of the team's achievement generates much happiness. I can feel it from here. Everyone in the

Circo starts to sing the national anthem. The BBC has cut away so all I have is the sound by phone. As the players and the multitude sing together '*Fratelli d'Italia . . . L'Italia s'è desta . . .*' I hear Valeria singing along, too, and her voice is cracking with emotion.

postscript

My journey started with a double proposition: that the World Cup is a kind of universal, shared story for our age, and that football is a form of storytelling in its own right.

After recovering, but before returning to Rome, I ran into an old friend in London. We talked about the tournament and he surprised me by saying he had been disappointed by the World Cup: 'It's like Christmas. The best part is always the build-up. Then it starts and you think: "Oh, but it's just blokes playing football." This is the flipside of the experience of Valeria, who knows nothing much about football yet found herself swept up by the excitement of Korea and of Italy's triumph. For both of them the game itself was secondary; what counted was the peripheral stuff, the anticipation, the pleasures of feeling connected to others in crowds.

But that begs the question of why it is that, among all

sports, only football produces these reactions around the globe? Why not fencing or dressage or even baseball? Part of the answer is surely that football meets so well Hollywood director Sam Fuller's famous definition of another type of universally popular narrative, the movies. Fuller said: 'Cinema is like a battlefield: love, hate, action, violence, death. In one word, emotion.' Emotion was what made Poland, Italy, Korea, Japan and Argentina fun. And football clearly follows at least some of the rules which film-makers, novelists and philosophers all tell us apply to telling stories.

Like all good drama, good football has its vivid protagonists and antagonists (Zidane and Materazzi, for example). Great drama has conflict at its core; conflict is the very essence of the game. Our pleasure as spectators derives in large part from our identification of and with archetypes, heroes, villains, comic characters, tragic figures, and so forth.

We are free to interpret the stories of football in any way we choose. The fact that different people may draw completely different meanings from the same events simply highlights the power of the story. (No Italian, for example, would agree with me about Grosso; in Italy he is an unsullied hero.) But it's the fact that football works as a story that makes football important. Stories, after all, are the way we make sense of the world and our place in it. Stories are the basis of all civilisations. All nations, all peoples, all groups, all families everywhere on earth at every time in history have defined themselves by the stories they share. At the dawn of Western storytelling, Aristotle told us how dramas must have a beginning, a middle and an end. Football does that. Aristotle also said that drama requires unity of time, place and action – and the game adheres firmly to that principle too (audiences can be anywhere, of course).

Yet many football matches are, frankly, dull. Why is that? Well, probably for the same reason that many books, films and TV shows are dull. They simply fail to deliver the storytelling goods. The action is flat, the characters boring, and the story doesn't develop in any interesting manner. Just like Ukraine–Switzerland.

Before I set out, I wondered if football would seem different in every place. Would the rituals of people watching football in different countries be different or the same? The answer is, of course, both.

This book is crammed with examples of differences, some culturally determined. As the Korean professor told me: 'The world is getting smaller but east is still east and west is still west. Because we share more and more things doesn't mean we become the same.' In Gdańsk, Irena, who was as passionate about the game as anyone, responded to defeat by breaking out the vodka and dancing on the table. In Buenos Aires, the mourning involved stunned silence and 1,000-yard stares. How different can you get? On the other hand, there was much more that united each crowd that clustered around a TV set everywhere than divided them. Wherever in the world I was, as soon as a TV game started, I entered a shared space wholly outside geography. The rituals of football are simple but profound. They enact dramas that resonate deeply with almost every human on the planet. Nobody has satisfactorily explained quite why this should be so. But, as football audiences grow ever greater, as its cultural, social, political and economic impact burgeons, we should recognise at least that the capacity of the game to tell us stories is making it a global language.

ACKNOWLEDGEMENTS

Heartfelt thanks to everyone who helped me before and during my journey, especially Henk Spaan, 'Hard gras', the Dutch Fund for Special Journalistic Projects and Evelyn Fishburn.

My especial gratitude to those who so generously put me up on my travels:

Árpád von Klimo and Eva Thumshirm (Berlin), Tore Persson and Shuting Gao (Stockholm), The Kay Family: Alan, Andy, Sue, Michaela and James (Vancouver) and David Bourne in Washington, DC.

A NOTE ON THE AUTHOR

David Winner is a freelance journalist. His books
include *Those Feet* and *Brilliant Orange*.
He lives in Rome.

A NOTE ON THE TYPE

The text of this book is set in Bembo. This type was first used in 1495 by the Venetian printer Aldus Manutius for Cardinal Bembo's *De Aetna*, and was cut for Manutius by Francesco Griffo. It was one of the types used by Claude Garamond (1480–1561) as a model for his Romain de L'Université, and so it was the forerunner of what became standard European type for the following two centuries. Its modern form follows the original types and was designed for Monotype in 1929.